'Would you like to be buried with my people?'

'Would you like to be buried with my people?'

Irish Wedding Traditions

Kerstin Mierke & Bridgette Rowland
Illustrations by Jeremy Purcell

NONSUCH

First Published 2007
Copyright © in this edition 2007
Nonsuch Publishing Limited

Nonsuch Publishing Limited
73 Lower Leeson Street, Dublin 2, Ireland
www.nonsuch-publishing.com

British Library Cataloguing in Publication Data.
A catalogue record for this book is available from the British Library.

ISBN 978 1 84588 571 7

Typesetting and origination by Nonsuch Publishing Limited
Printed in Great Britain by Oaklands Book Services Limited

Contents

Foreword

I have never had a wedding, unless you count the time I was wearing my First Holy Communion dress and pretended to my 'walking up the aisle' partner that we were, in fact, getting married. He started crying and told the priest that he was scared. I was given a new Communion buddy – a fierce-looking child in dungarees who tried to bite off the Bishop's finger as he handed out the holy bread. A wedding is different to a marriage. Weddings are a great laugh, full of beautiful dresses, nervous giggles and delicious cake. Some marriages end, and it's awkward for the two people involved. All weddings end, of course, but some leave a much sweeter aftertaste. Being a part of an Irish wedding is possibly the most fun you will ever have. The first things that spring to mind are copious amounts of alcohol, badly applied fake tan and, of course, two people who love each other. They must love each other enough to stand outside a church on a freezing day, in between two warring mothers, and still manage to smile and look gorgeous in the photographs.

If you are brave enough to have a real Irish wedding then this book will give you some wonderful ideas as well as make you laugh out loud at some of the old stories and traditions. The authors tell of what went on before the current traditional wedding, in the days that preceded the Celtic Tiger. The days when houses were a fiver, and a man was only a man if he had a few acres (by a few, I think we all know that two is too little and a herd of cows is no less than six breeding heifers and a lively bull). Some of the stories you'll have heard before, such as the scary race to the altar before the baby is born, so as to avoid the rigmarole of telling curious 1950s neighbours exactly how the child was born weighing fourteen pounds, yet was two months premature!

Most of us are familiar too with the adorably quaint matchmaker. I've never seen an actual matchmaker or a leprechaun but I guess they look quite similar. I've always imagined a matchmaker to be a tiny, nosey man with a cap and a magic stick. They are still in existence today in some parts of the country according to this book, though largely replaced by dating agencies and the internet. I do not really have advice to give except for this. In these modern times, we are all very busy but you must never agree to get married to somebody unless you have met them a few times. At least discuss what type of wedding you want.

Weddings in Ireland generally follow the same pattern. Months in advance, while the wedding is in the planning stages, the bride-to-be looks at her groom-to-be in a special way – with a cool smile and knowing eyes. This is her way of explaining to him that his input into the planning will be, at best, barely tolerated. She is the Bride and therefore knows exactly what is needed to make the wedding a triumph. Many ladies are born with a tiny switch buried deep under the skin of their ring finger. This switch leads to their brain via their heart, and can only be activated by placing an engagement ring on said finger. It is the Wedding Day Switch and cannot be ignored.

Once the switch is on, the lady is in full preparation mode. There are thousands of things to sort out for the wedding day!

Will she invite vegetarians? Will her dress be ivory/cream or cream/ivory? What about the honeymoon – is Spain so last year that people would laugh, or so last year that it'll be trendy again by June? Will her best friend spend just enough time in the gym to look alright but not so much that she looks better than the bride? These are very different worries to the concerns of past brides. A long time ago, brides and their bridesmaids would all dress in identical dresses for fear that the fairies would come and steal a standout pretty girl. That is unlikely to happen now, in fact it sometimes seems that the bride deliberately dresses her bridesmaids in unflattering dresses on purpose! Perhaps some brides think empire-waisted salmon frocks with mauve lace are adorable – who's to say? Past brides have also been subjected to playful 'kidnapping', which sounds like slightly less fun than getting a cocktail stick in your eye. The American tradition of smashing wedding cake into each other's faces is not likely to catch on here, we value our confectionary too much. Our mothers would go mad at the thought of the cleaning, too. Different traditions appeal to different people; some think garters are naff but others couldn't be married without them. I say, don't throw them out into the crowd, keep them and use them as a hairband. That way everyone will know you are married! Brides must throw the bouquet, this is supremely fantastic. Nonchalance is feigned by the unmarried ladies for about eight seconds, then all hell breaks loose and it is a sight to behold – or even partake in. Always remember – a wedding makes a wedding. If you are a single person then learn from the strawboys of old. You must gatecrash every wedding in your local community, invitation or not. You must then wink at the priest three times; this is another old superstition that is said to help you find your new husband or wife, albeit one I made up myself.

This book is a great antidote to the serious list-making and stress of wedding planning, it will make even the most professional bride take a moment to have a giggle!

I'm not a veteran wedding-goer, but the ones I have been to have been joyful, funny affairs, full of family and friends of the two people taking those somewhat scary vows. The best bits are the slightly wonky bits, like when the flower girl tries to eat the confetti and the best man tries to save his speech after misjudging the mood and saying something slightly off-colour. The best time is always near the end of a wedding, when the brand new husband and wife look at each other across a gigantic drunken crowd of badly dancing loved ones and start to laugh together.

Maeve Higgins
2007

Introduction

Whether you have just gotten engaged, are already married, or are single, it is very difficult to go through life without getting swept up at least once, or multiple times for that matter, by the craziness of a modern-day wedding: cakes several storeys high, meringue-style dresses, limousines, stag nights, hen parties, the cacophonous symphony of honking car horns … caught up in this whirlwind of confetti, the modern wedding is a world unto itself. But, like any world, it has a rich history that has shaped and moulded its present identity.

What we're about to embark upon is a contemporary look at our wedding heritage. History and folklore form the backbone of this book, but just because something is in the past doesn't mean that it is not still very relevant to our present. This book is an attempt to blow the dust and cobwebs away and introduce modern-day brides and grooms to their historic counterparts.

Before any wedding can take place there are two essential ingredients: a bride and a groom. But in the past, before dancehalls and nightclubs became the middle ground for courting couples, how did men and women meet and romances blossom? We take it for granted nowadays how much easier it is to meet members of the opposite sex. We attend college together and share workplaces. At night we venture out with our friends to pubs and nightclubs and occasionally catch the eye of a member of the opposite sex as we strut our stuff on the dance floor. And if all else fails, we can always try and meet our match in cyber space. However, in the past people generally didn't stay in school past the age of twelve, never mind attend college. Men and women occupied different spheres of the workplace and it was frowned upon for women to frequent public houses. To make matters worse, unions were often dictated by economics rather than love, with both men and women conscious of the need to make a good match and keep poverty at bay. Matchmakers introduced couples and negotiated the bride's dowry, dances were held at crossroads and young men wooed their sweethearts with Celtic knots and sweet nothings. The Irish dating scene of old was fraught with obstacles, but where there is a will, romance will find a way.

Single men and women turned to divination customs for reassurance that they would eventually find love. Using charms, potions and a host of other methods, they tried to summon the name or face of their future partner. If he/she was already known to them, then they would cast spells over their beloved to inspire a requited love. These practices were not exclusive to women, and men were often to be found at the helm of the cauldron.

Being single was once comparable to being a leper in Irish society. In the past, women received the brunt of the discrimination. They were called old maids – a term we tend to tiptoe around today. An unmarried woman was not considered a fully fledged member of society – her single status was seen as a handicap and she was partially excluded from the community. On Chalk Sunday, which happened once a year, the community had an opportunity to make its feelings known by branding the single people with a stripe of chalk and generally chastising and tormenting them for the day. This is one custom I'm sure many people weren't sorry to see the back of.

Various superstitions surrounded every aspect of wedding preparation, and the wedding day itself. There were certain days of the week and months of the year that were deemed lucky or unlucky for marriage. Irish people were so terrified of fairies that they had a whole host of tricks up their sleeve to outwit these little people. The wedding dress, the threshold, horseshoes, the bouquet, the journey to the church, the first dance – every single feature of the wedding was accompanied by a litany of dos and don'ts, that if strictly adhered to were said to guarantee a lifetime of wedded bliss. Some of these superstitions live on today, whilst others have evolved in unison with the changing times.

Wedding fashions have changed dramatically over the centuries. The white wedding is thought to be the be-all and end-all of wedding fashion, but it only dates back to the nineteenth century when Queen Victoria started the trend. Before this, red tunics and petticoats, miniskirts and the bride in a man's suit all enjoyed their heyday. The evolution of bridal fashion has been, as fashion tends to be, exciting and unpredictable.

When the bride and groom finally made it up the aisle the words 'I do' were only the start of the fun and festivities. With the alcohol flowing freely, the groomsmen played pranks on the groom, strawboys gatecrashed the reception and the bride and groom's wedding night was thwarted by friends intent on ruining the mood with their fun and games. Honeymoons were rare and couples were sent crashing back to reality with a bang on the day after the ceremony.

It is possible to honour old customs and have a traditional Irish wedding without it being too twee and overrun with leprechauns and shamrocks. The above traditions can be interwoven with a modern-day wedding and the following pages will show you how to do so. Food, flowers, church decorations, the garter, hen and stag parties and the ceremony itself are all discussed in detail, with suggestions as to how you can endow them with a touch of tradition. However, Irish weddings in the past were so jam-packed with superstitions and traditions that trying to incorporate them all could result in one very frazzled bride. So it is probably best not to take it all too seriously and not to get too obsessed with superstitions – after all, in recent years no brides or grooms have mysteriously disappeared with fairies being the prime suspects.

We hope that this book will help you navigate the corridors of olden-day weddings and acquaint you with the rich heritage your ancestral brides and grooms have handed down to you. As you mingle with the ghosts of weddings past, we hope that not only do relations run smoothly, but also that perhaps a little something from the past can pave the aisles of weddings yet to come.

Chapter 1

Matchmaking and Dowries

The Economics of Love

> Woman seeks man with good-sized farm and several livestock.
> Good personality and good looks not essential.
>   — Mary (can supply good dowry)

If Irish men and women of the nineteenth and early twentieth century had been blessed with such a wondrous tool as a personal ad then the above is what the average one might have looked like. In contrast, ads in the twentieth century are more likely to resemble the following:

> Woman seeks tall, dark and handsome man with larger-than-life personality and wallet to match.
>   — Chantelle (leggy blonde)

Matters of the heart are as complex today as they were in the Ireland of the nineteenth and twentieth century. However, their backdrop has changed dramatically. Where now we have internet-dating sites and speed-dating events, we once had matchmaking and dances at the crossroads. Where issues such as partners being separated by distance or demanding careers now prevail, different social standings and levels of income once tore young lovers apart. When one equation is solved, another equally complicated one generally presents itself. However, one of the greatest differences between Ireland today and Ireland of yore is the element of choice. Today, people regularly post personal ads searching for their perfect, tailored-to-fit partner on a sale-or-return basis. People shop around in order to find their exact match – and rightly so. Relationships in the past were fuelled by a host of issues. There was a strong emphasis on the family and division of land, and marriages were often determined by one or the other. Economic bargaining was pivotal to the formation of a relationship and if the price wasn't right then there was simply no deal. That is not to say that there weren't a great deal of happy unions to be found and that romance didn't play its part. It was just that society presented people with a limited number of potential suitors who were not always the most compatible. Sayings and proverbs abounded at the time, giving an indication of the common attitude held by people:

A pot was never boiled by beauty.

She mightn't be much to boil a pot of spuds but she'd look lovely carrying them to the table.

The general consensus seemed to be that love, whilst it would be an added bonus in a relationship, wasn't going to put bread on the table. If a man had a nice temperament and was easy on the eye it was often a stroke of luck. But if he had several pigs or cattle to his name a woman had struck gold. Ireland of yore had its own version of our present-day dating websites and personal ads,

in the shape of matchmakers and go-betweens. They helped facilitate matches between couples of equal social and financial standing and this equality was of particular importance to the respective families, the silent partners in the marriage. It was acceptable to marry within or above your station, but to marry below it was ill-advised. However, lest one should think that marriage in those days was all doom and gloom, the matchmaking process provided some comic relief. Fun and games abounded and parties and celebrations were commonplace, with dancing and singing until all hours of the morning, and an obligatory bottle of whiskey or poitín doing the rounds. From dowries to eating the gander, and walking the land to all-night parties, the dating scene was a roller-coaster ride all the way to the altar.

Society in the nineteenth and early twentieth century afforded very few career opportunities for women. There were only a very limited number of avenues available, such as going into service or becoming a teacher, and women looked to marriage as their main hope of financial independence from their parents. They simply traded in one set of financial benefactors for another. However, the life of an old maid was extremely undesirable. Society disapproved of unmarried women and unmarried men alike. An old unmarried woman was awarded less respect by the community than an eighteen-year-old married woman. Marriage was a rite of passage and, once a couple had settled down, their status in the eyes of others was greatly enhanced. Whereas women were under pressure to marry so they could leave their parents' home, men on the other hand were under pressure to provide an heir for their farm. Women were not usually tied down by such constraints as inheritances and were free to marry as soon as they found a willing groom. But a man's marriage prospects lay at the mercy of his mother and father. He might have to wait until their death before he inherited the farm and had the means to support a wife. In the event of his parents living to a ripe old age, he might be in his forties or fifties before he would be able to marry. Relinquishing control over the farm was a very big deal for parents – it reduced them to a state of dependency and left them with no voice or authority in their own home. Some men married for love, some to provide an heir and others simply to find a replacement mother figure to cook and clean and pamper them (so some things never change no matter how much time elapses!).

Unfortunately, then as now, an unmarried woman past her prime was far too quickly relegated to the infamous shelf, whereas an unmarried man was forever looked upon wistfully as an eligible bachelor just looking for the right woman to tame his wily ways.

As much as society has evolved and the battle of the sexes is now being fought on a more even battleground, men have always seemed to sit more comfortably with the title 'bachelor' than women do with the far less flattering 'spinster'.

It's a Boy/Girl!

The ritual of marriage originated with a view to protecting children. Children were central to marriages in olden-day Ireland and unfortunately the responsibility weighed heavily on the woman's shoulders. Not only was she given an uneven share of the work involved in rearing them, but if she failed to get pregnant in the first place the blame lay solely at her feet; it never crossed anyone's mind that the macho bread-winning husband might be accountable. In some cases dowries were paid in several instalments: the first half was paid on agreement of a marriage and the second half on the birth of the first child – evidence of how important it was for a woman to be able to bear children. On the other hand, if a woman gave birth to all girls and no boys, this too was seen as a failure. Men wanted an heir to pass their farm onto, who would keep the family name alive. If a woman's husband died early in their marriage when she was still childless, she might be returned to her family. If her father had had the foresight to only pay the first half of the dowry upon marriage, he might be able to provide for her with the remaining half. Before the advent of modern machinery, farms were very labour intensive and children were seen as a future work-force (alongside being bouncing bundles of joy of course!). When women weren't busy giving birth and rearing their children, there was a host of other domestic duties to occupy them. If a woman didn't have a large dowry to recommend her in matrimony, perfecting her domestic skills might boost her attractiveness. Cookery, sewing and farming skills were worn like a badge of honour by young women. Upon marriage, a mother-in-law was expected to pass over the running of the household to the young bride. Nowadays, with the existence of such inventions as washing machines, dishwashers and microwaves, our kitchens practically run themselves. We are entrusted with the not-so-challenging task of flicking a switch. But olden-day brides spent their days ticking off an endless list of time-consuming chores. A woman who could darn a sock or turn her hand to some farm work was seen as compensating for what she lacked in terms of material possessions.

Girl Power

Nowadays 'Girl Power' seems to be the mantra of the female gender with young girls proclaiming it loudly like a super-power (often before they even understand its meaning). Where we now have female presidents, it wasn't so long ago that women didn't even have the vote. Women have been empowered; liberated from age-old shackles they are now encouraged to pursue their dreams. In the past, women had very little power and played a passive role when it came to their love lives. The dating scene was very much the man making the moves and the woman demurely accepting or rejecting his advances. There was, however, one day every four years when women were allowed to wear the pants in the relationship. On 29 February every leap year, women had twenty-four hours in which they could propose to the man of their dreams. This custom was known as the 'Lady's Privilege'. There are many theoris about its origins and actual practice.

Some believe that a woman was free to propose on any given day of the leap year, whilst others believe it was restricted to the 29th. If the man refused he had to offer a forfeit. This varied from sums of money to expensive items of clothing or household goods – a small price to pay for shattering a woman's dreams. An enterprising woman could have used this day to her advantage and turned over a handsome profit by proposing to various men she was confident would refuse her – but if a man accepted she risked finding herself in a very awkward situation. This tradition is said to date back to the time of St Patrick and St Brigid. St Brigid was upset that men had the monopoly over marriage proposals and she resented the fact that women were assigned such a passive role. To placate her, St Patrick offered her 29 February as a concession – though one day every four years hardly seems like the most generous of concessions. So for any women reading this, who are tired of waiting for their partner to propose – get out your calendar and check when the next leap year falls and take control of your own destiny. Or better still, make every day of every year 29 February and, dare I say it, disregard tradition.

In the absence of nightclubs, men and women had to find other means of socialising and meeting members of the opposite sex. As travel was difficult, the dating pool was largely restricted to one's immediate locality. Young people who grew up together usually had parents and grandparents who had also grown up together, so that everyone knew one another within a radius of several miles. The downside of this was that within that same radius many people were already related through marriage and there was a realistic fear of inbreeding within small communities.

Matchmaker, Matchmaker, Make me a Match

Dance halls didn't appear on the scene until around the 1950s. Before this, people held dances in their own homes and in the open air at crossroads. Whilst men frequented public houses, it was considered most un-ladylike for a woman to do so. Unlikely events such as Mass or harvest time provided potential mating grounds where many a match was made. However, some Irish farms were in remote, sparsely populated areas, making it difficult for the inhabitants to meet members of the opposite sex. Where couples didn't come together of their own volition, matchmakers were on standby to lend a helping hand. An area might have up to three or four practicing matchmakers. They were usually male, in fitting with the matchmaking process in general – women being relegated to the sidelines. The ideal matchmaker was one who followed the vocation as a hobby rather than as a career and so was motivated by a desire to make good matches rather than purely by financial gain. Matchmakers were well-connected within their community and sometimes within neighbouring communities, which could help alleviate the problem of inbreeding. Their peak season was from October to Easter Sunday, during which period most marriages took place. Payment was usually in the form of a bottle of whiskey or poitín or a small sum of cash. There were many different names given to the matchmaker: cosherer, *spréicéirí*, bowthies or speakers. An unofficial matchmaker was often called a blackfoot. The business of making matches was no cushy job. A matchmaker's reputation was constantly on the line and if he made one bad match, word could spread. Various factors had to be carefully analysed. The obvious question of whether or not a couple were economically compatible was of primary importance.

But a good matchmaker would ideally take the compatibility of temperaments and personality traits into account. Unfortunately, it was not uncommon for matches to be made between men of sixty years or more and girls in their teens. In fact, until the introduction of the Marriage Act of 1972, girls as young as twelve and boys as young as fourteen could legally get married.

The first attempts to pair a couple usually took place between the matchmaker and the father of the bride over a pint in the comfortable setting of a public house. If a matchmaker wasn't involved, the discussion took place between a relative of both parties. Markets or fairs also proved popular places to broach the subject. It was an informal way of gauging the level of interest the other party had in the match. However, despite the casual setting, the proposal would have been premeditated and all the pros and cons of such a match would have been carefully weighed up. When a matchmaker made a house call to suggest a potential match,

he always came armed with a bottle of whiskey or poitín. The alcohol helped loosen tongues and made both parties more open about what they wanted from the match. However, there was a common saying at the time that 'Many fellows brought the whiskey and never got the woman.'[1] Negotiations would take place as to the size of the dowry and other technicalities such as the matchmaker's fee, how many livestock and acres of land would be included in the bargain and where the groom's parents would take up residence. The bride in question might be forced to listen in silence as her marriage prospects rested upon whether or not her father would relent and concede an all-important extra pig to the dowry. The bride was usually already acquainted with the groom if he was from her area but there were cases where they only met for the very first time on their wedding day. Peig Sayers, famous for her autobiography *Peig*, did not meet her husband Pádraig Ó Gaoithín until the day of their wedding. Pádraig was a native of the Blasket Islands and he whisked Peig away from her family and out to the island as soon as they were married. Not only was she marrying a stranger but she was being completely uprooted from her life as she knew it. However, she claimed to have lived a very happy life with Pádraig nonetheless. But it definitely can't have been easy arriving at the church oblivious to who was going to be greeting you at the altar – and a sly retreat back down the aisle wasn't really an option if you weren't happy with what you saw.

The Dowry

The question of the dowry was the main sticking point in negotiations. Dowries were usually paid by the bride's family to that of the groom in cases where she was marrying into a farm.

There were occasions, however, where the opposite occurred and the bride, perhaps not having any brothers, would inherit her father's farm, and any man wishing to marry her would have to 'buy' his way in. The ancient Celts had a similar tradition called the 'bride-price' whereby a suitor would shower a woman with gifts of various sizes in exchange for her hand in marriage. Dowries were either paid in one lump sum or in several instalments. The advantage of paying in instalments was that it was a temporary form of insurance. If the bride failed to produce an heir, she might be sent back to her family and the remaining unpaid dowry would be used to provide for her. Dowries were calculated based on how much each party stood to gain from the marriage. The more cows/ sheep/horses a man had, the nearer his holding was to the road, or the more acres he had, the more he could ask for. This meant that marriages generally took place between people of equal ranks in society; a poor woman would not be able to afford the dowry needed to marry a wealthy man and a wealthy woman would rarely bestow her fortune upon a penniless man. Negotiating a dowry could be a long, drawn-out affair with both parties finding it very difficult to reach an agreement. If a woman had very little money, it didn't matter how attractive or charming she was besides, without a dowry she would find it hard to attract a suitor. On the other hand, an unattractive woman, both physically and in character, with a large dowry, would have her choice of men.

Unfortunately, many individuals paid little heed to the old saying, 'The dowry drops over the cliff but the drooping lip remains on the wife'. The bright lights of America attracted a lot of Irish women. Lured by stories of the 'American Dream' and streets paved with gold, many women emigrated and went into service there. Some married and had families, never to return, but others saved up every cent they earned and put it towards their own dowry so that they would eventually be able to attract a suitor back home. After long periods of time, sometimes ten years or more, they returned to Ireland, having traded their youth in for a husband. Members of a family who emigrated to America sometimes sent what little money they could afford home to contribute to the dowry of a sister. The groom's family would in turn put a dowry to good use. It might cover the fare of a sibling to America or be used as a dowry for a sister marrying into another family. Alternatively, it was invested into the improvement and expansion of the farm. Dowries could be anywhere in the region of £50 or more, sometimes amounting to several hundred pounds, which in those days would have been a small fortune. The present-day tradition of the bride's family paying for the wedding stems from this custom of paying a dowry to the groom's family.

Walking the Land

Once the dowry had finally been agreed upon, a tradition known as 'walking the land' took place. This was to ensure that the farm was exactly as described by the father of the bride or groom, and that the poitín consumed during the initial talks hadn't induced wild delusions of grandeur. As every pig, cow, or acre of land laid claim to increased the dowry accordingly, it was important that all the assets be verified. It was not unknown for families to borrow livestock from a neighbour for the day in order to make the farm look more impressive and to back up their wild claims. Many matches were called off on the basis of the farm having one fewer pig than originally stated. If the couple were in love it must have been quite tragic to be torn apart over something so trivial. Once the farm had been investigated and the surveyor was content with what he saw, great celebrations ensued. This was known as 'eating the gander'. It took place in the house of the bride-to-be. A goose was killed and served in honour of the occasion and music and dancing went on until all hours of the morning. The legal technicalities were ironed out the following day. A solicitor from the nearest town was present while both parties signed what were known as 'bindings'. The dowry, either in full or in part, was entrusted to the solicitor.[2] With a down payment secured, the betrothed couple now simply had to await their big day.

Romance

The dating scene in olden-day Ireland can at times seem very clinical and more like a business transaction than the culmination of a whirlwind romance. The Irish people are far from the top of a 'Most Romantic Nation' list, with the likes of the French probably laughing at them from their lofty vantage point. Irish men are sometimes mocked for handling their pint of Guinness more tenderly than their girlfriend or wife. But, ironically, one of the greatest figures in the history of romance is buried in Dublin. The remains of St Valentine, the famous saint after whom St Valentine's Day is named, were entrusted to Whitefriar Street Church in the 1900s by Pope Gregory XVI.

Irish men were capable of bouts of romance when the mood struck and many courtships involved some good old-fashioned wooing. Men offered their sweethearts Celtic knots as a symbol of their love. The knot dates back to the fifth century when it was used by the ancient monks to illuminate the renowned *Book of Kells*. The knot is infinite – with no beginning or end it represents never-ending love.

Runaway Brides

Elopements and abductions were a last resort for some couples. Runaways often occurred when a dowry couldn't be procured and a union was opposed by both sets of families and the community at large. The couple might elope and marry in secret or alternatively simply remain away for long enough so that on their return their parents would be forced to consent to the marriage. It wasn't uncommon for a couple to use an elopement to blackmail the bride's father into increasing the dowry. It was assumed, and usually unfairly, that the woman returned from an elopement no longer a virgin. Her parents would then readily consent to a marriage as their daughter's reputation hung in the balance. Unsurprisingly, many men harboured feelings less pure than those of true love when they eloped with a woman. Although it was frowned upon for the man not to make an 'honest woman' of her, if he chose not to the scandal would eventually subside and he could easily marry in the future; the woman on the other hand was tarnished for life in the eyes of potential suitors. In the nineteenth and twentieth century, Ireland was very conservative and pre-marital sex was (and still is) forbidden by the Church. There was, however, a custom known as 'bundling' that enabled men and women to share a bed outside of wedlock. It was all very innocent, however, and couples would generally just cuddle up together and go to sleep. However, the Church strongly condemned this tradition and so it was not widely practiced.

Women weren't always willing participants in elopements. They were sometimes abducted in merriment or even against their will. The Terry Alts were a Catholic body whose aim was to protect tenants and land labourers from landlords and bailiffs. However, in many places they took the law into their

own hands and were ruthless and reckless in their behaviour. In the days of the Terry Alts, women were regularly abducted. Sometimes the Terry Alts were working on behalf of a third party. A local farmer might hire them to abduct a girl so he could force her to marry him. Other times the Terry Alts acted independently and abducted whichever unfortunate girl took their fancy. Many women married at a young age rather than leave themselves at risk of being abducted by a Terry Alt. In instances where a girl resisted the abduction, she was branded on the left side of her face with a red-hot iron in order to disfigure her and reduce the chance of any other man ever wanting her.[3] The Terry Alts reached a peak around the middle of the nineteenth century after which they gradually began to disappear.

Apart from the occasional elopement, young people had a deep-rooted fear of marrying without the approval of their parents and the community. At the time, Ireland was very superstitious and many believed that a wedding that didn't have the blessing of family and friends was doomed from the outset. The announcement of a wedding was headline news and every second person had their tuppence-worth to give. Today, Ireland is a melting-pot of different cultures and people come together in marriage from opposite corners of the world, as well as opposite corners of Ireland. However, in the nineteenth and early twentieth century, couples had often grown up together in the same small community. This meant that not only would their parents be acquainted, but their brothers and sisters might also be friends or foes. Such an interlinked history could unfortunately spawn many problems for a relationship. Perhaps the two fathers had once fallen out over the sale of livestock, or a brother from either family might have had a childish squabble in the playground that had never been resolved. When a couple decided to marry, their two families were essentially merging too, and the transaction did not always go smoothly. On the other hand, such claustrophobic settings could also prove advantageous. If a bride or groom had any negative attributes or a shady past it was usually well known and the other person was fully aware of what they were getting themselves into. Today, with the popularity of the faceless internet-dating phenomenon there is a lot to be said for knowing someone's history!

The Dating Scene Today

Arranged marriages began to die out around the 1950s with the advent of the dance halls. However, Ireland still has two official remaining matchmakers. Willie Daly of County Clare is one of these, and he proudly claims to be a third-generation matchmaker. Alongside his daughter Marie, he carries on the tradition. According to Willie, the essential tools of a matchmaker are 'intuition, subtlety, gentle nudges, a little encouragement, the right atmosphere and insightful knowledge of human nature'. Willie is conscious of the fact that many people consider his service old-fashioned but he argues in defence of the tradition:

> We know that the matchmaker's job became obsolete when people, especially women, gained more independence and participated to a greater level and with greater frequency in all echelons of the work force. Cultural and economic changes consequently occurred and lo and behold the matchmaking tradition was no longer required. Then life became too hectic, and people became too busy and too particular to meet each other and fall in love, hence the birth of the computerised dating agency. While we recognise the success of the dating agency, we ourselves do not believe in the statistical approach to finding love. We believe in the old and natural methods.

Willie is not alone in his efforts to sustain this old tradition. The town of Lisdoonvarna, also in County Clare, holds an annual matchmaking festival every September and October. In the past, farmers would gather in the town after the crops had been harvested. They were eager to find a wife with whom they could pass the dark, lonely winter that stretched out ahead of them. The festival is now a major event and draws huge crowds every year from all over Ireland and abroad. The matchmaking festival ends with the bestowal of the coveted titles of Mr Lisdoonvarna and the Queen of the Burren. In keeping with the times, the matchmaking events have evolved into such modern interpretations as speed dating. However, Willie Daly makes an appearance to reconnect the festival with its traditional roots. There is no walking the land or eating the gander at this festival and I am fairly certain no dowries exchange hands, but nevertheless you just might get lucky and meet your match.

Aside from a few lingering ties, the tradition of matchmaking has died out in Ireland. Arranged marriages still take place to a small degree amongst the Travelling community. This is more out of a desire to keep the bloodline pure than because of economic motivations. But here too the tradition is disappearing. There is a fine line between matchmaking and arranged marriages. Love can oftentimes be a lottery with the odds stacked against you, so having someone narrow the playing field a little can improve your chances immensely. However, the element of choice is essential. So perhaps with a few tweaks here and there, the abolition of the dowry and maybe a picture of the prospective spouse at hand, the tradition of matchmaking might just make a comeback.

Chapter 2

Divinations, Love Charms and Love Spells

Good morrow, good yarrow,
Good morrow to thee,
Please help me this night,
My own true love to see.
Show the clothes he wears and his
Hair let me see
And tell me right truly if he will wed me.

The Irish have never been a passive race when it comes to matters of the heart. Ironically, despite the fact that they had very little control over whom they married, they whiled away the long evenings mixing love potions, reciting incantations and trying to ascertain who their future love would be. Perhaps these divination customs gave them the illusion of having more control over their love lives than they in fact had. It was mainly women who delved into the occult but men, on occasion, were known to fall prey to the same romantic follies.

The following pages contain various divination methods, love charms and potions specifically for the aid of he/she who has yet to find their partner. But be warned – you practice them at your own peril. Some of these customs require crossing over the very thin line that separates the physical world from that of the spiritual. So tread carefully. Seeing the face of your future partner can come at a high price and if the devil demands your soul in exchange then perhaps you ought to reconsider the bargain.

Methods of Divination

Divination was primarily used where a person already had a lover in mind and simply wanted to know if their feelings were reciprocated and if they would, as hoped, one day be wed. However, there were times when no such attachment had yet been formed and young people looked to the various divination methods to discover if they would indeed be married at all.

Snails

On May morning, before sunrise, go out to the garden and the first snail you see take up and put it on a plate sprinkled lightly with flour, place a cabbage leaf over, and so leave it till after sunrise, when you will find the initial letters of your lover's name traced on the flour (this can be done between two plates as well). Should the snail be quiet within his house when you take him up, your lover will be rich; but should the snail be almost out of his shell, then your future husband will be poor, and probably will have no house or home to take you to when you wed him. Therefore, take good heed of the warning given to you by the snail, or avoid trying your future fate if you are afraid of the result.

— Lady Wilde, *Ancient Cures, Charms and Usages*

Snails are not usually the first creature to spring to mind when one thinks of wisdom and divine foresight but Irish people of yore invested a lot of faith in these small, slimy creatures. It is also interesting that a man's wealth was so integral to this divination practice. Snails clearly must have had more of a nose for sniffing out material assets than personality characteristics such as compassion or sincerity. However, at a time when poverty had such a strong grip on the nation, having a roof over your head and food on the table was of primary importance. But it is still hard to believe that some people may have actually taken the word of a snail above the cries of their own heart.

'The Drutheen'

'The Drutheen', which is supposed to possess the power of revealing the name of a sweetheart, is a small white slug or naked snail, and it is the common practice of boys and maids on May morning to place one on a piece of slate lightly sprinkled with flour or fine dust, covering it over with a large leaf, when it never fails to describe the initial of 'the loved name'.

— T.C. Croker, *Fairy Legends II*

Snails and slugs carried a huge burden of responsibility upon their shoulders (if snails and slugs had shoulders, that is). Nowadays, many men would like to think themselves too macho for a lot of divinatory practices and some women, on the other hand, might be too squeamish to handle these slithery, slimy creatures. However, maybe we underestimate slugs and snails and our ancestors recognised in them a hidden and divine talent. Or, then again, maybe not! But if you are willing to get your hands a little slimy then there is only one way to find out.

Ashes

Among others it is thought right and proper to have the threshold swept clean on May-Eve. Ashes are then lightly sprinkled over it, and in the morning the print of a foot is looked for. If it turn inward a marriage is certain, but if outward then a death will happen in the family before the year is out.

— Lady Wilde, *Ancient Cures, Charms and Usages*

Nowadays you might get a few funny glances from family members if you're sprinkling ashes all over the floor but in the past this was quite a popular method of divination. People might pore over a footprint for hours, trying to convince themselves that it was turned inwards and not outwards, however much evidence to the contrary. In the end, it might transpire that the footprint did not belong to the ghostly incarnation of their future spouse at all but to a thirsty family member who had simply stolen downstairs for a glass of water during the night. However, where no interference was apparent, this divination practice could be the source of either a great deal of happiness or a great deal of upset.

Nuts

Two hazelnuts, walnuts or chestnuts, or even two grains of wheat, were selected and named after some boy and girl who were supposed to be courting. They were then placed side by side on a bar of the grate, or in the turf-ashes, and according to whether they burned quietly, or jumped apart from one another, so would be the future before them. Four plates having been set down on a table, water was poured into one, a ring placed on another, some clay in the third and in the fourth was placed either some straw, salt, or meal. A person would then be blindfolded and led up to the table, and into whichever plate he or she placed their hand, so would their future turn out. The water signified migration, the ring marriage, the clay death, and the fourth plate prosperity. On re-arranging the order of the plates others would be blindfolded and led up in like manner.

— William J. Fielding, *Strange Customs of Courtships and Marriage*

This divination practice incorporates some of the main preoccupations of our ancestors. Would they be forced to emigrate? Would they get married? Would they live a long life? Would they have enough money to make ends meet? Perhaps a modern-day version could be modified slightly. The ring could still signify marriage but perhaps the clay could be representative of new life in the form of children, the water could represent extensive travels abroad and the straw/salt/meal could represent a successful career.

T'Burn Nuts on a Holl'Eve

First dry them well, and then let them burn on a hot griddle, or on a bar i' the grate, iv it's broad enough; or on the hearth stone. If they burn up t'wan another, that's a sign the couple 'ill be married, but if they jump away, the pigs 'll run through it. If they go out soon, they'll not be longlivers; a' if wan o' them blazes over tother he'll be very proud ov her. If the big nut o' one pair burns up toarst the wee one ov another pair, it's leckly meeby that a widda man 'll marry a widda wumman.

— Billy McGart, *Poor Rabbin's Ollminick for the Town of Belfast*

For anyone who didn't quite catch that, this divination custom involves assigning a pair of nuts (hazelnuts or chestnuts for example) the names of the couple in question. By placing them in the fire you could predict the outcome of the couple's relationship based on the way the nuts burned. If they burn silently your love will be faithful and steady; however, if one jumps away from the other the love will not be reciprocated. This may seem like quite a random method of divination on which to be basing all your hopes of future happiness, but the idea behind all these marriage divination customs was that a higher force was at work and you simply had to place your faith in this divine intervention.

One of the most popular divination customs, which has survived unto the present day, is performed on All Hallows Eve and requires a barmbrack. The following objects are mixed into the dough: a ring, a thimble, a button, a silver coin, a religious medal, a chip of wood and a rag. Each object holds significance for the future of its finder:

Ring: Marriage
Thimble: A life of domesticity
Button: Bachelorhood
Silver coin: Wealth
Religious medal: Holy orders
Chip of wood: Domestic abuse
Rag: Poverty

Nowadays, this tradition has been downsized and it is normally just the ring that is included. This is probably a good thing on two accounts – firstly it makes for easier chewing not to have to be on the look-out for quite so many hard objects and, secondly, not having to face the prospect of a future life of domestic abuse makes for a much happier Halloween.

On Halloween, the dish colcannon was also used for the purpose of marriage divination. Colcannon is a mixture of mashed potatoes and cabbage. A wedding ring was included in the mix. Boys and girls would then gather around the large dish and gulp it down as fast as they could, each eager to be the first to discover the ring. This tradition often resulted in a few severe cases of indigestion. And on occasion, in all the haste, someone might unwittingly swallow the ring.

Halloween was a very popular time for divination as it was believed that on this date the physical and spiritual worlds drew closest together and ghosts and apparitions could pass over into the physical realm. In *Bealoideas*, Cáit Ni Bhradaigh notes the following tradition:

On Hallowe'en a young unmarried girl would place three knots in her garter and at each knot recite the following incantation:

This knot, this knot, this knot I see
The thing I never saw yet,
To see my love in this array
And what he walks in every day
This night may I in my dreams see,
And if my love be clad in green
His love for me it is well seen,
And if my love be clad in grey
His love for me is far away,
And if my love be clad in blue
His love for me is ever true.

The woman then places the garter under her pillow and that night she will dream of her groom-to-be.

Another tradition still commonly practiced is that of putting a piece of wedding cake under your pillow. It is said to inspire dreams of your future marriage partner.

Other Methods of Marriage Divination

- If you stand in front of a mirror at midnight and recite the appropriate incantation then your future husband will replace your reflection in the mirror.
- If you manage to peel an apple in one unbroken piece, throw it over your shoulder and let it fall to the ground. The skin should fall in the shape of the initials of your future spouse.
- Drop a ball of woollen thread into the pit of a limekiln and wind it back slowly. If the string catches, the girl asks who is holding it and the voice of the future husband will answer.
- Write the letters of the alphabet on individual pieces of paper. Float these face-down in a basin of water. In the morning they should be found to have sunk to the bottom and those which have turned over to show the letters, will show the initials or spell the name of the future spouse.
- Hard-boil an egg and remove the yolk. Fill the cavity with salt and eat it whole. Go to bed without saying another word or letting a drop of liquid wet your lips. Your future partner will appear to you in a dream and offer you a drink to quench your thirst.
- Wash your face before bed but do not dry it. Your lover will then appear to you in your dreams, offering you a towel with which to dry yourself.

Love Charms

Love charms were commonly recited over food and drink. It was thought that magic entered the bloodstream much faster if ingested and it would produce a very powerful effect. Whilst preparing food for her man, a woman can recite the following to strengthen their bond:

The charm Mary put on her butter
Is the charm for love and lasting affection:
May your body not cease
To pay me attention
May your love follow my face
As the cow follows her calf
From today till the day I die.

Whilst preparing a drink for her beloved a woman can recite the following love charm three times:

> *This is the charm I set for love,*
> *A woman's charm of love and desire,*
> *A charm of God that none can break,*
> *You for me and I for thee and for none else,*
> *Your face turned to mine,*
> *And your head turned away from all others.*

And finally, for any men that may be feeling left out, here is a love charm especially for them. If a woman isn't responding to a man's advances he must search for a raven's feather and make it into a quill. Pricking the tip of his ring finger he must use the blood to write the following verse:

> *By the power of Christ brought from*
> *Heaven, may you love me, woman. As the*
> *Sun follows its course, may you follow me.*
> *Like light to the eye, meat to the hungry,*
> *Joy to the heart, come and stay with me,*
> *My beloved, until death do us part.*

Love charms were usually strongly worded. Nowadays, the expression of such sentiments might send any man or woman with the slightest hint of a commitment-phobia running for the hills. With the words 'till death do us part' being a common ingredient, some might even say these charms hint at an obsessive and unhealthy love. The people who cast them would most likely disagree. But if these charms succeed and you turn your beloved into a love-struck puppy dog then you will be well-matched in obsessiveness and more than likely live happily ever after – till death do you part.

Love spells

Many of the older women in a community were well-versed in concocting love potions and were in great demand with the younger generation. But in order for them to work, the woman for whom they were intended needed to be the one to actually cast the spell. Love spells, whilst quite common, were also greatly feared. People were happy to be stooped over a cauldron themselves but they were terrified of ever being the subject, or rather the target, of such magical forces. On rare occasions marriages were even terminated upon the discovery that one of the parties had resorted to such trickery prior to the romance.

Friday is the optimum day for casting a love spell as it is believed to be the day that rules romance. Incense is believed to have powerful romantic effects. So if you are looking to create a particular mood with your beloved then you may want to consider the following different types of incense:

Copal: helps reconcile differences
Gardenia or Lavender: heals wounds inflicted by love and brings peace and happiness
Jasmine: increases luck in love and relaxation and confidence
Musk: increases sexual desire and arouses passion
Nutmeg: enhances physical and magical energy
Patchouli: for a happily-ever-after love affair
Rose: for pure love

Violet: stimulates love and brings luck and protection
Ylang-ylang: strengthens love and increases sexual desire

Different coloured candles are said to have powerful healing effects on a relationship. So if you happen to be experiencing difficulties then not only can you cure a whole host of problems by lighting candles, but you will also score brownie points for being romantic.

Green: fertility, marriage and prosperity
White: peace and purity
Peach: joy and strength
Blue: happiness, healing, tranquillity and truth
Orange: attraction, joy and stimulation
Yellow: imagination, communication and creativity
Pink: affection, harmony and romance
Rose: enhancement of a relationship
Red: energy, love, passion, sexual potency and strength
Purple: success, spirituality and wisdom
Black: repels dark magic and negative thought-forms

Spell for Lasting Love

By candlelight, put a lock of your own hair and that of your beloved into a hollowed-out gourd. Add powdered unicorn root and dried pansy petals. Hold the gourd over the smoke of frankincense and myrrh incense for a period of five minutes then cover it in white fabric and bury it in your garden. This spell will ensure lasting love.

Spell to Inspire Passion

To increase the levels of passion in your love life, light a red candle and fill a red flannel or silk mojo bag with dried rosebuds and rose petals (for female energy), cinnamon (male energy), mandrake root (for fertility), and a piece of garnet or rose quartz. Carry this bag with you at all times.

Spell for Requited Love

Ten leaves of the hemlock dried and powdered and mixed in food or drink will make the person you like love you in return. Also keep a sprig of mint in your hand till the herb grows moist and warm, then take hold of the hand of the woman you love and she will follow you as long as the two hands close over the herb. No invocation is necessary but silence must be kept between the two parties for ten minutes to give the charm time to work with due success.

— Lady Wilde, *Ancient Cures, Charms and Usages*

In Anthony Bluett's book *Ireland in Love*, he speaks of an unusual manner of inspiring affection that may not agree with the stomachs of some readers:

> Another means of attracting the affection of a man was to catch a frog, put it in a box and bury it alive in a bank or dry ditch; when the flesh of the frog withers to the bare skeleton, pick the bones apart and select a certain bone; the next step then was to secretly insert this bone in the clothing of the victim with the result that he or she will fall madly in love with the person who had placed the bone there in the first place. The victims of ministrations such as these were not entirely without means of defence, however, for there were a number of measures which could be taken in order to counteract their effect. One particularly useful method was to cut off a bit of the hair of the girl in question, burn the hair and feed the ashes to the young man, mixed in with his tea or food.

Perhaps women of yore had stronger stomachs than women today. Nowadays, most women would no more like to see a frog nor touch it, than have to handle its rotted carcass. But I suppose desperate times call for desperate measures and perhaps at the root of this practice was a subconscious hope that the frog might turn into a Prince Charming and the woman would be spared the latter half of the spell. However, as if frog bones weren't bad enough, there was another spell that involved a woman boiling the excrement of a white gander and getting her beloved to drink it. A man wishing to cast a spell on an unsuspecting girl had to substitute the excrement of a gander with that of a black chicken.[4] One has to wonder if perhaps a bouquet of daisies and some chocolates might not have been just as effective.

To Destroy Love

If the object of a woman's affections loved another, there were certain ways and means of coming between the lovers.

- If the woman could procure a piece of clothing belonging to the man's lover she could cast a spell that would turn the man's feelings from love to hatred.
- A jealous woman could take a handful of clay from a newly dug grave and shake it between the couple whilst saying, 'May ye hate each other like Christ hated sin or bread eaten without invoking His blessing.'
- When the priest asked the bride the all-important question, a jealous woman could mutter 'I do not' under her breath whilst knotting her handkerchief.

Frog bones, a gander's excrement, snails, apple peels and hard-boiled eggs – Irish people of old had quite an eclectic range of tools with which to try to manipulate love to their own advantage. There is very little information on record as to whether or not any of these methods were in fact successful but there is only one way to find out.

* The authors accept no responsibility for any adverse affects that may occur during the administration of the above customs, e.g. the consumption of a gander's excrement.

Chapter 3

Shrovetime and Chalk Sunday

In the past, Irish weddings usually took place during wintertime. Summer weddings, despite the fine weather they promised (although in Ireland this is a promise that is rarely kept), were uncommon, with most weddings occurring during the long, cold winter months. This was especially true in rural areas where life revolved around the farm. Walking up the aisle took second place to picking potatoes and turning hay. However, farm work came to a standstill during the winter months and it was during the long, dark evenings that the matchmakers began to plot and scheme, young girls daydreamed about knights in shining armour and men went down on bended knee. The countryside was awash with Romeos and their Juliets forming an orderly queue to the altar. One of the most popular days for a wedding, in the entire calendar year, was Shrove Tuesday. It marked the beginning of Lent and, traditionally, no marriages took place during these forty days and forty nights. Lent was a time of abstinence and penance. A wedding celebrated during this time, complete with a feast, dancing, drinking and merriment wasn't really in keeping with the story of Jesus' hardship in the desert. Shrove Tuesday was the ideal day for a wedding as it was the last day on which people could indulge and enjoy their few luxuries before the period of abstinence began. Shrove Tuesday also marked the beginning of spring – a time of renewed growth and hope as the icy face of winter melted from people's memories.

Chalking

As the evenings started to grow shorter the pressure to marry began to mount for the young single men and women in an area. People had ample leisure time during the winter and so married people made a sport out of prying into the affairs of the younger people in the locality. Some acted as self-appointed matchmakers, trying to coerce unions where possible. The build-up to Shrovetime was the busiest time of the year for a matchmaker and his services were eagerly sought out. Marriage wasn't really seen as a decision in those days but rather as part of a natural course of events. It was believed that people *should* marry and some people found it impossible to comprehend why anyone would not wish to. To actually choose not to get married was considered a gross negligence of one's social duties. Community members saw it as their duty to promote the sacrament of marriage. They helped encourage unions through the innocent game of chalking that took place on the aptly named Chalk Sunday. The unmarried were singled out and branded like sheep, with large stripes of chalk adorning their clothes. Children and adults alike lurked in the shadows, a piece of chalk in hand and their victims clearly identified. The cries of the unmarried went unheard as their clothes were mercilessly covered in huge, glaring stripes of neon chalk. Resistance was futile, as it only heightened the fun for the aggressors and increased their determination. Repeat offenders were the favourite target, as they were seen as a challenge and new methods of 'breaking them down' were constantly being devised. The younger men and women found it easier to force a smile and take the joke in good spirits as there was always next year and the hope that they might still find a partner. However, for the older single people each passing year saw their smile grow fainter and the likelihood of them staying indoors for Shrove Tuesday increase dramatically. In the west of Ireland there was a tradition of sprinkling salt on bachelors and spinsters in order to 'preserve' them until the following year.[5] On occasion, Chalk Sunday fell on the Sunday before Shrove Tuesday rather than the first Sunday of Lent. Men and women were decorated with chalk as usual but a glimmer of hope lay in the fact that there was still time for them to find a match, woo him or her and then march them swiftly up the aisle in time for Lent. Such was the pressure and desperation created by Chalk Sunday.

These pranks were a source of great amusement to the people enacting them but beneath their innocent exterior lay a more serious motive. It was hoped that chalking would encourage people to marry, if only to avoid being the butt of such pranks year in, year out. Nowadays, we may not get covered in chalk but many people have found themselves the victim of that busybody aunt/grandmother/neighbour, who over the years seems to wait for major social events to repeatedly ask you when you're going to give them a 'day out'. However, as the years pass, this (still very public) question may evolve into 'And it's a shame you never got married', thus pronouncing their judgement on your future marriage prospects (and obliterating any hopes you may still have been harbouring). But with a piece of chalk in hand that irksome relative or neighbour would be rendered all the more deadly.

'So you're off to the Rock'

For those who were not married by Shrove Tuesday, there was always the option of getting married on the island of Sceilg Mhicíl. This monastery seemed to be a world unto itself, exempt from the Church rules of the mainland. Easter was celebrated here a month later, and bachelors and spinsters, for whom the events of Chalk Sunday had been too much, could safeguard themselves against the following year's devilment by making haste to the next boat. Taunts of 'You're off to the Rock I suppose?' followed closely at their heels. Numerous other pranks surrounded this tradition. The phrase 'You're damned if you do and you're damned if you don't!' springs to mind. Names of the couples making the trip were compiled into a list which was then put up all over the town. The unfortunate couples were exposed in a much more efficient manner than through the time-consuming practice of chalking. For every list that was torn down another was put right back up. Local poets and writers put pen to paper to write catchy little poems and ditties rhyming off the names on the list amidst humorous tales of high tides and stormy seas as they made the perilous journey to Sceilg Mhicíl. Sung to a catchy air the songs lodged in your head like a pop song and the community went around humming the names on the list for days and weeks on end. A game was made of matching potential couples and guessing who would be stepping off the boat hand-in-hand with whom. Even though these trips were embarked upon as a result of all the pressure to marry, rather than applaud the couples the community saw the voyage as penance for not having married sooner.

All the marriageable young people, men and women, in any parish, who are not gone over to the majority at Shrovetide, are said to be compelled to walk barefoot to the Skellig rocks, off the Kerry coast, on Shrove Tuesday night; and have also to bring back home blocks of bog-deal or bog-oak as penance for the misdeed; the amount of the load to be in proportion to their offence. Thus a young man or woman whose 'first offence' it was, was said to be 'let off light', but henceforward the offender was said to be 'loaded' in proportion to her or her contumacy.[6]

In south-east County Cork there was a tradition known as 'Going to the Skelligs', whereby married men went around the community on Shrove Tuesday evening searching for unsuspecting bachelors. The unfortunate man they stumbled upon would be bound with rope and have his head soaked under a pump or ducked into a well as punishment for his single status. On occasion, he might even be thrown into a pond.[7] The first Sunday after Shrove Tuesday was known as *Domnach na Smuit*, or Puss Sunday in some places. The unmarried were said to arrive at Mass with frowns so long they trailed after them as they shuffled into the church. The community interpreted their distraught expressions as disappointment that they had not wed but it is more likely that they were simply distressed at the thought of all the pranks and devilment that awaited them that day.

Depending on what side of the fence you were on, Chalk Sunday could be the most fun you'd have all year or the most fun other people would have at your expense all year. Chalking was the equivalent of burning a scarlet 'S' for 'single' onto the cheeks of the bachelors and spinsters. Nowadays, being single is more multi-faceted. There will always be the nagging aunt who wants her big day out but there are others who see a certain amount of independence and freedom in not getting married. Marriage has become more of a personal choice rather than one we are herded into at the wielding of a piece of chalk.

Chapter 4

The Wedding Day

Fundamentally, modern-day weddings haven't changed that much from those of the eighteenth and nineteenth century – sure, the dress may now cost the bride an arm and a leg whereas in the past her Sunday best may have sufficed, or honeymoons might now be to the opposite corner of the globe whereas the best room in the bride's house was the exotic destination of yore. But the simple words 'I do', were, and still are, embedded in a whole host of preparations, traditions and partying. In the past, however, this was done on a much smaller budget. Whole communities might be in attendance and so it was very important for the family who was hosting the reception in their home to have the place in tip-top condition, with ample food, drink and music to impress the critics. Sympathetic neighbours would often give food to the family to help minimise expenses. Nowadays, wedding receptions are held in all kinds of venues, from medieval castles and five-star hotels, to Baywatch-style beach strands. In the past, the reception was traditionally held in the bride's home. Guests would spill out into the adjacent barn if space became an issue. Weddings were held early in the day and the reception was known as the 'wedding breakfast'. True to Irish form, drinking and dancing would go on into the early hours of the morning. Today, some weddings are on such a grand scale that a whole team of employees may be drafted in to help plan and organise the event. In the past, aside from the odd society wedding, people simply didn't have the time or the money to invest in finer details such as special napkins or chocolate-fondue fountains. Instead, they entertained their guests in a more humble and economical fashion with an array of games and devilment.

Marriage Banns

It was, and still is, legally required for the bride and groom to give three months' notice of their impending nuptials. In the past the marriage banns were announced at three consecutive Sunday Masses when the majority of the community would be gathered together. The reasoning behind this was to allow anyone who might object time to form their argument and it also gave the couple themselves time to reflect on their decision. Such marriage laws are common across the globe. However, the infamous State of Nevada in the United States caters for 'shot-gun weddings', allowing a couple to get married immediately after the question has been popped. Funnily enough, this state also has one of the highest divorce rates in the world. In the past, marriage banns prevented people from rashly entering into a union that could prove near impossible to get back out of again. Divorce wasn't a readily available option so couples had to be confident that they were making the right decision.

Blame it on the Weatherman

When the wedding day finally arrived, the weather conditions helped determine more than just whether or not to bring an umbrella. If the day dawned bright and sunny it was considered a good omen for the future of the marriage. Alternatively, if it was overcast and raining, future hardships were foretold. It was also lucky to hear a cuckoo on the wedding morning, or to see three magpies. The journey to the church in the nineteenth and early twentieth century was undertaken on foot. Therefore, many of the elaborate trains we see on wedding dresses today would have been highly impractical. A mud-splattered bride does not paint a pretty picture. The tradition whereby it is bad luck for the groom to see the bride before the wedding is relatively new and, in the eighteenth century, wedding parties would set out for the church together, with the bride and groom towards the front, and a piper leading and keeping the party entertained. Alternatively, the bride would travel on horseback, with her father at the helm on the way to the church and her new husband in the saddle on the way home. It was considered unlucky to meet a funeral on the way to the church. Up until the early nineteenth century the ceremony was usually held in the bride's home. This was on account of the Penal Laws of 1695, which made it illegal for Catholics to practice their religion in public. These laws were finally abolished in the 1820s but the tradition of home weddings lingered on for some time after that.

Rings and Things

Wedding rings, whilst an important part of the ceremony, were a huge expense that crippled the bank balances of many an eighteenth- and nineteenth-century couple. The more affluent members of society could afford gold or silver rings, but peasants might have to make do with pieces of straw or wood fashioned into a circular shape that might remain intact for the day if they were lucky. A far cry from the diamond-encrusted engagement rings of today but, diamond or straw, the sentiment was exactly the same. Claddagh rings came into fashion around the eighteenth century. They consist of two hands clasping a heart, surrounded by a crown. The ring belongs to a larger group of rings called 'Faith Rings'. There are several stories attributed to its origins, one of the most famous relating to a man named Richard Joyce who came from a small fishing village called Claddagh in County Galway. Legend has it that pirates captured him and sold him into slavery shortly before he was to be wed to his sweetheart. His master was a rich and skilled goldsmith who noticed Richard's aptitude for the craft and trained him as an apprentice. Whilst in captivity, he became a skilled craftsman of precious metals and set about designing the perfect ring. His captor became so attached to Joyce that he offered him the hand of his most beautiful daughter in matrimony. But Richard turned her down.

In 1689, King William III ascended to the English throne. He sent one of his subjects to Algiers to demand the immediate release of all British captives. Richard Joyce was a free man again. He returned to Galway to find that his fiancée had waited for him. He proposed to her with the ring he had designed

– representing the three essential ingredients their union encapsulated: love, friendship and loyalty. Whilst some cynics might find this story nauseatingly romantic, it has, nonetheless, helped to sell an infinite number of these rings worldwide. The different ways of wearing the ring indicate the status of your heart. If you are single you must wear the Claddagh on your right hand with the bottom of the heart pointing out. If you are in love but not married you wear it on your right hand with the bottom of the heart pointing inwards. And finally, if you are engaged the ring is to be worn on your left hand with the heart pointing inwards. The Claddagh is often handed down by mothers, from generation to generation, to their first-born daughter.

With the advent of photography, couples became keen to capture their Kodak moments. However, in the early stages of the technology, cameras weren't quite as mobile as they are today and so couples would have to travel to the home of the photographer as opposed to taking pictures at the actual wedding. This was usually done several days before the big day. The couple would get dressed up in their wedding finery and pose as a newly married couple. Many pictures from this period show heavily bearded men as it was said to be extremely unlucky for a woman to marry a beardless man. Doing so would lead to the early death of her parents, so the groom would often grow a beard for the occasion if he did not already have one. A little bit of facial hair was a small price to pay in exchange for the health of his in-laws. It is thought that the custom of grooms sporting beards dates back to the time of tribes in Ireland when all the chieftains and warriors would have been well endowed (with facial hair that is!).[8]

After the Ceremony

When the ceremony was over the fun and games began. The newlyweds were showered with rice as they left the church. This tradition was predated by the pagan tradition of showering the couple with grain. Pagans believed that the fertility of the seeds would bode well for a 'fruitful' union between the couple. Rice symbolises luck, abundance and immortality and ensured fertility in the union. It was also said to feed evil spirits and distract them from inflicting any harm on the bride and groom. The modern-day equivalent of this tradition is the throwing of confetti. It is said that a man should always be the first to wish the bride luck after the ceremony. It was bad luck for a woman to be the first to do so. Unfortunately, jealous women sometimes made it their mission to be the first to reach the bride. Perhaps they had been jilted in love or left on the shelf themselves and resented anyone else enjoying the marital bliss they had been denied. Gunshots were traditionally fired into the sky in celebration of a union but, unfortunately, the odd bullet inevitably went astray and bullet-shot wounds have a tendency to steal the limelight from even the most beautiful of brides. Nowadays the hooting of car horns is the much safer version of this tradition.

The journey to the reception was plagued by games and pranks. The bride and groom would travel home via a different route than that which had been taken to the church. There were two reasons for this: firstly it was said to symbolise the new path they were embarking upon in their married life and, secondly, it was a means of outwitting their mischievous friends who had several tricks planned for the journey. Kidnappings and abductions were a constant threat, along with the tradition of 'roping'. This was where the groom's friends barricaded the road so that the wedding party couldn't get by. Their passage would only be permitted on payment of a 'toll'. Another common tradition was the 'bottle race'. The groom's friends would compete with one another for the prize of (no surprises here!) a bottle of whiskey or poitín. As grand demonstrations of strength and endurance they would embark on horseraces at break-neck speeds, all driven on by the distant smell of alcohol.

The Reception

When the entire wedding party were eventually assembled at the bride's house, the reception began. The meal usually consisted of cabbage, turnips and bacon, washed down with porter, poitín or whiskey – a far cry from today's menus that offer an array of choices and as many as five courses. Good-natured neighbours would lend cutlery, crockery and pots and pans to help cater for the wedding party. The couple ate salt and oatmeal at the beginning of the reception as it was thought that this concoction would protect the couple from the 'evil eye'. Meade was also served at weddings. It was made from honey, water and yeast. It was thought to encourage virility in men and fertility in women. Some couples would continue drinking the concoction for weeks after the wedding, so strong was their faith in its effects. This is thought to be where the word 'honeymoon' is derived from. The wedding cake was a very simple affair. In the eighteenth century it was a sweetcake made of oatbread but, as the decades and centuries passed, it multiplied in tiers and eventually matured into the miniature skyscrapers we see at some weddings today.

As soon as the last plate had been cleared, the music and dancing began. Polkas, reels and hornpipes set the dance floor ablaze. The oldest man and woman in the house were called upon to dance the *an port Deàbhaltach* (the Devil's jig). Various musicians serenaded the wedding party throughout the night, with the piper usually taking main stage. It was considered unlucky for either the bride or the groom to sing at their own wedding. However, they were given free reign of the floor for their first dance together as a married couple, a tradition that is still practiced today. It was imperative, however, that the bride keep one foot on the floor at all times for fear the fairies would gain control and spirit her away. The fairies seemed to have a preference for brides over grooms but, just to be on the safe side, it was recommended that grooms unbutton one button on the leg of their pants to protect them from any harm at the hands of these mischievous little people. The priest was the guest of honour at weddings – after the bride and groom of course. A collection was made to cover his fee for the ceremony.

A hat might be passed around and people would donate what little they could. Alternatively, the priest was sometimes in charge of cutting the cake and the guests would pay a small sum in exchange for a slice.

The Strawboys

Wedding crashers were a frequent feature of nineteenth-century weddings. Weddings were generally quite small as families simply couldn't afford the expense of feeding such large numbers. Communities were so close-knit that there were always individuals who would be insulted by their exclusion. Lured by the food, drink and festivities, they pondered long and hard how they could arrive uninvited and still be made feel welcome – and so the strawboys were born. Wearing conical hats, masks and capes, all made of straw, they concealed their identity and gatecrashed the wedding reception. A certain amount of skill was required in making these straw suits as they needed to be resilient enough to withstand the vigorous dancing enjoyed during the night, as well as the wandering hands of guests intent on exposing their identities. They often carried sticks with them to fend off such unwanted advances. The night was considered a failure if the mask of even one of the members was to slip.

Strawboys went by several other names including soppers and ragamuffins. They travelled in groups of a dozen or fewer. They usually included a *sean bhean gáirteach* (a laughing old woman) and a *sean fhear saibhir* (a wealthy old man). The members were selected on the basis of their ability as performers and many of them were very talented singers, dancers or musicians.

Their appearance at a wedding was thought to bring the bride and groom good luck in their future life together. The leader usually wished the bride luck before asking her to dance, whilst the other members were partnered with the bridesmaids. At the end of the dance the leader of the strawboys placed a crown of straw upon the bride's head.

They met with mixed reactions – they were uninvited yet they were not unwelcome. If strawboys didn't show up at a wedding it was seen as a bad omen, so their presence was tolerated and they usually stayed no longer than about a half hour. Not only were they considered a good omen but some people saw them as representative of the wider community's approval of the marriage. Strawboys could have several weddings to attend in one week and often left one wedding to attend another the very same night, so great was the demand.

It was very important that the wedding party treat the strawboys with the utmost respect and hospitality. They were usually paid a small fee for their appearance and to placate them, for fear they would grow rowdy and play pranks. They might be paid with money or receive ample food and drink instead. If they were made to feel at all unwelcome the good luck they represented would quickly turn sour. They would throw their costumes up into the trees and leave them there to rot to symbolise the bad luck they wished upon the couple in their future married life.[9] On the other hand, if they felt they had been well treated they unmasked and made a bonfire of their costumes in the yard.

Nowadays, this tradition has more or less died out. On occasion, however, some wedding parties arrange for friends and family to dress up and adopt the role in honour of the old days. However, for anyone not familiar with the tradition, the appearance of these strangely clad folk can cause quite a stir. After all, straw masks, hats and skirts are not in fitting with the average wedding's dress code. But a little bit of disruption and hi-jinks is a small trade-off for the lifetime of happiness they promise the newlyweds.

Gifts

Neighbours gave wedding presents in the form of helpful donations for the reception, such as food and crockery. However, local businesses sometimes gave gifts of full sets of china, delph or pictures. The gift was often part of a hidden agenda. It was a way of procuring loyalty from the bride and encouraging her not to take her business elsewhere on entering the groom's family. There were no wedding lists for guests to resort to or suggested 'favourite' stores of the bride and groom in which to shop like nowadays.

Handmade quilts, or other such items, were often given as presents that would prove useful to a young woman settling into her new home. They complemented her treasured bottom drawer. The bottom drawer was the term given to a collection of household items that a woman had been gathering and hoarding since she was a young girl. It was also known as a 'hope chest'. It was full of items that would be useful for when she was setting up her own home, such as linens, napkins and crockery.

The Long-Awaited Wedding Night

Wedding parties tended to go on until the early hours of the morning. At some point during the night the newly married couple would attempt to sneak off to bed unnoticed. However, their every move was being carefully monitored by their friends who weren't going to be denied a few more pranks before the night was out. The marital bed was an easy target and anything from frogs to clay could be bedding down with the new couple for the night. Pre-marital sex was strongly condemned by the Church so the bride and groom might be very nervous about their first night together. In some cases, where the marriage had been an arranged one, they may have only met for the very first time that day. The words 'I do' might have been amongst the first they ever exchanged. Added to their nerves was the consciousness that the whole wedding party was watching their every move, awaiting their bedtime, amused by the young couple's trepidation. Not content to end the pranks with a few frogs in the bed, the perpetrators would crowd around the door to the bedroom whilst others fought for space outside the window. They would sing loud and annoying songs, bang on the door and tap on the window until they tired themselves out.

All in all, the newly married couple's first night together wasn't always set against the rose-tinted, romantic backdrop they might have envisioned.

Chapter 5

After the Wedding Day

The morning after the night before, the bride and groom awoke to their new life together. Upon opening the bedroom door, several of the couple's late-night tormentors, having fallen asleep at some stage during the previous night's devilment, would come tumbling into the room and awake with a jolt. No doubt the man received the odd pat on the back and the woman the odd raised and inquisitive eyebrow, as they sat down to breakfast and the start of the rest of their lives together.

No Rest for the Wicked

Honeymoons are quite a recent wedding tradition. In the eighteenth and nineteenth centuries there were no bargain Ryanair getaways and transport in general was very limited. The more affluent couples might be able to afford a temporary respite from reality on a holiday within Ireland but for the working class it was often a case of going back to work the following day. As most weddings took place in February or March, the new farming season was just getting underway. The groom, if he was the eldest child in his family, would officially be handed over the farm immediately after the wedding. His new bride would be expected to swap her wedding dress for overalls and wellies and to row in with the rest of her new family.

Hauling Home

The couple were transported to the groom's house in a tradition known as 'hauling home'. They travelled on horseback and were flanked on all sides by the bride's new neighbours. The verb 'hauling' conjures up an image of a heavy load as the bride was removed, roots and all, from her old life and planted firmly in her new one. Traditionally the hauling home was only done on a Friday, making Thursday the optimum day for a wedding.

If a wedding took place on a Friday the couple would have to wait nearly a full week before they would be transported home. Despite the rarity of honeymoons and the fact that a couple often had to face back into farm labour immediately after the wedding, the parties and celebrations continued as soon as the sun set. Often the neighbours or friends of the groom threw these parties as a way of welcoming the bride to the community and also just as an excuse for prolonging the festivities.

The New Abode

There are numerous traditions surrounding the bride's arrival in her new home. Crossing the threshold is accompanied by several superstitions. It was customary for a piece of delph, no matter how expensive or inexpensive, to be broken before the bride crossed the threshold, as a good-luck omen. The groom is also supposed to carry the bride across the threshold and into her new home. There were several reasons for this. The first explanation dates back to Roman times when it was thought to be unlucky for a bride to stumble upon entering her new home, so the groom carrying her was a preventative measure. There are no stories of grooms stumbling, though one can only assume that this would have been a doubly bad omen. So for any men reading this – tread carefully! The second explanation is that the threshold was thought to be the boundary where demons lay in wait for the bride, so the groom would gather her in his arms and carry her to protect her from these evil spirits. He would then place her in front of the hearth as it was the symbolic heart of the house. There was another tradition whereby the bride's mother-in-law would crumble a piece of cake over her head as she entered the house – another portent of good luck both for the marriage and future relations between the groom's mother and her daughter-in-law.

The bride was not allowed to return to her parent's home for a full month after the wedding. This was known as *Mí na Meala,* or the Month's Mind. It was hoped that this month of enforced separation would encourage the bride to adapt to her new home rather than running home to her old and comfortable way of life at the slightest hiccup. When the month was up the bride visited her parents on what was called Monthly Sunday and her return sparked great celebrations. The new couple would not attend Mass in the parish on the Sunday after the wedding. This tradition is said to date back to the time when landlords considered it their right to bed a new bride. They would kidnap her and hold her ransom in their house for a period of several days or more. If the groom attended Mass during this time without his new bride, the community would assume that the landlord had claimed his prize. It was a cause of great embarrassment for both the bride and the groom. As time went on, a tradition evolved that all newly wed couples would refrain from attending Mass on the first Sunday after their wedding. This was an act of solidarity that safeguarded everyone's reputation in the public eye. The following Sunday the couple made their first public appearance on what was known as Shine Sunday. They were accompanied by the bridesmaid and the best man and they were all dressed to impress. Standing in the pew the couple were the subject of many sidelong glances and hushed conversations as the community carefully dissected them. Having made their deductions, the community decided whether or not they would embrace the couple with open arms. A new bride also had to beware of the evil eye. She was at particular risk upon her first public appearance after the wedding. She would naturally attract a lot of attention within the community and in case someone were to make a 'bad eye' at her it was recommended that she wear something that would deflect this negative attention. It was thought that an unusually beautiful item of clothing, or an equally ugly one, would attract the eye and the bride herself might go unnoticed.

When the Confetti Settled

The post-wedding parties eventually petered out and the couple settled into a routine. Up until 1973, women in most professions were forced to give up their jobs once they were married. For many women this was incredibly difficult. They were stripped of all financial independence and forced to rely upon their husbands for everything. If a woman was unlucky enough to marry a stingy man, she faced an uphill battle all the way. She might find it difficult to get money from him to buy food for the household, never mind a penny extra to spend on herself. Some women carried out small jobs on the side such as dress-making, which generated a modest income, allowing them just a sliver of glorious independence. Whereas a man's life didn't change that drastically after marriage, for women their whole worlds could be turned upside down. If their husband was from another locality they faced complete upheaval, having to leave all of their family and friends behind in the move. They were expected to take over the running of the new household as well as having to pitch in with the farm work. Unfortunately, for some women the household signed over to them sometimes came complete with one very unpleasant mother-in-law who could make life difficult for her new daughter-in-law. Instead of rejoicing at having gained a daughter, as the old saying goes, they instead resented her and saw her as having stolen their precious son away. The daughter-in-law replaced the mother in both her central role in her son's life and in her household as well. The mother-in-law was expected to surrender the running of the house to this new woman but she didn't always give up without a fight. However, neither woman had an easy transition to make. In some cases, the poor bride also got several of the groom's siblings in to the bargain. The groom's family might not have anywhere else to go and so would continue living in the family home. The bride might be expected to cook and clean for everyone. When a wife wasn't chained to the kitchen sink she found that her position in society as a whole had changed dramatically. The 'Mrs' now preceding her name meant that people addressed her with much more respect. In turn, she was expected to adopt a demeanour that complemented her new level of respectability. Any remaining vestiges of her girlish and immature days were to be cast off and replaced by a more sober air, befitting of a married woman. On the other hand, there were many women who took great pride in being housewives and excelled in the domestic sphere. They adapted quickly to married life and embraced all the changes it brought.

In olden-day Ireland, in the absence of a career ladder for women to climb, it was expected that having and rearing children would be their profession. It was inconceivable that a woman might not be in possession of a motherly instinct or that she might decide to postpone having children until later in life when she felt she had lived enough of her own life. Children were the expected outcome of marriage and the Catholic Church forbade the use of contraception. This meant that not only did women often become pregnant very early in their married life, but no sooner had they given birth to one child than they were pregnant with another. A woman might spend the first ten to twenty years of marriage in a near-permanent state of pregnancy, meaning that having children became, literally, a full-time job. Families of ten or more children were not uncommon and such large families could be a huge financial strain. Some women tried to devise their own means of contraception, using methods such as *coitus interruptus* (also known as the withdrawal method) to try to control the number of children they had.

Ireland of yore was not quite as prim and proper as it might appear on first inspection. In Linda May Ballard's excellent book *Forgetting Frolic: Marriage Traditions in Ireland*, she addresses the issue of prostitution and sexuality in olden-day Ireland. Prostitution was common during the nineteenth century and men from all levels of society were more than happy to do their bit in keeping these women in business. Ballard makes reference to the idea of men as sexual aggressors whilst women were the passive sex, servicing the needs of their men but not getting any enjoyment from the act itself. She challenges this idea of the prudish, asexual woman with the following comical story of a bride from north Antrim who got married in 1739:

> We hear from Dunluce that a comical marriage lately happened there, between a couple from Finvoy near Ballymoney, as follows: the bride unfortunately happened to fall very drunk; who immediately after the priest had ended the ceremony, called out with a loud voice, *Go To Bed, Go To Bed*, and was heard at a considerable distance off, to the great shame of the bridegroom, who to prevent her cries and make her quiet, went to bed with her, but as she was going she fell downstairs and broke her nose. With much ado she got to bed, still crying *Go To Bed*, and the bridegroom having laid her down, went back to his company.

An arch wag then in the house took the opportunity of lying down with the bride in the bridegroom's absence, who, unhappily going to see his agreeable bride, found the honest fellow in bed with her in a very loving manner, which sight caused the bridegroom to fall into a swoon, while the arch fellow got off; the bride also got up and ran after him still crying *Go To Bed*, who fell down a second time downstairs and was thereby much hurt, having lost much of her blood. Her husband is in great trouble for the harm his spouse had so innocently met with.[10]

So perhaps present-day society and Ireland of old have more in common than one might first think. The main difference may be that nowadays sex is more explicit and socially accepted whereas, in the past, society demanded that one at least adopt a prudish public persona even if in private one was a raging nymphomaniac!

Magdalene Laundries

Women who were unfortunate enough to get pregnant out of wedlock were often forced into institutions for 'fallen women' known as Magdalene Laundries. They were usually admitted by a family member or the parish priest. In exchange for their keep they had to undertake hard manual labour in the laundries. These institutions were run by the Catholic Church and were originally set up to rehabilitate women who had worked as prostitutes. Alongside pregnant unmarried women, they also housed society's other 'undesirables', such as mentally challenged people. In some cases girls were admitted simply because it was felt that they were too flirtatious and that it was only a matter of time before they got themselves into 'trouble'. And apparently prevention is better than cure. Not surprisingly, there was no equivalent institution for men who were considered promiscuous. Women often suffered very harshly at the hands of the nuns. A girl's stay could be prolonged long beyond the birth of her child if she didn't have a family member on the outside willing to vouch for her. The last Magdalene Laundry in Ireland closed its doors as recently as 1996.

Till Death Do Us Part

Divorce or separation was only permissible in Ireland in extreme circumstances. If a man was found to have been violent or negligent towards his wife she might succeed in extricating herself from the union. However, this only happened on rare occasions and it would seem that a woman would, more often than not, choose to accept her lot, however awful it might be, rather than try to escape and have her dirty laundry aired in public. Women who drew the short straw on Halloween night and found a chip of wood in their barmbrack, might have wisely opted for the life of an old maid rather than risk entering into an unhappy marriage. If a woman divorced she was seen as second-hand goods by other potential suitors. And worse again, she would be demoted in society to a rank even lower than that of old maids, for divorcees were assigned the lowest rung on the social ladder.

Handfasting

The tradition of handfasting offered an alternative to couples who didn't want a Church or State wedding. It is an old Irish ceremony where a couple have the option of being bound for a year and a day, a lifetime or for all eternity. It was seen as a probationary marriage; a period during which two people could live together as a married couple and see if the set-up was to their liking. It was a step beyond betrothal but was still not as permanent as marriage. It wasn't usually legally binding, so either partner was free to walk away at any time. However, the ceremony could be made legally binding through the presence of an officiant with the necessary State qualifications. A couple also had the option of performing the ceremony themselves, without any witnesses. The tradition is an old Celtic ceremony that dates back to pre-Christian Celtic marriage laws. Under the sophisticated Brehon laws there was an understanding that marriages, though grounded in an ideal premise, didn't always work out in reality. People and feelings were subject to change and so 'forever' could indeed feel like forever if a couple began to regret their nuptials. Children, property and inheritances were all taken into consideration and in the event of a separation they were divided as equally as possible. These laws were very advanced, considering divorce was only made legal in Ireland, in certain circumstances, in 1997. Handfasting was based on a similar ideology to that of Brehon law. After a year and a day, if a couple decided they wanted to go their separate ways then they were free to do so. The year and a day they had spent together was the length of time necessary for a spouse to have a right to a share of property in the event of one of the partners dying. If children had been born then they were considered the equal offspring of the two parents. Both partners were then free to pursue other relationships and the handfasting ceremony was rendered obsolete. Normally, at the end of the year and a day couples opted for a long-term commitment and had a legally binding ceremony.

The handfasting ceremony involves the binding together of both partners' wrists with a length of ribbon or cord. The person performing the ceremony asks, 'Who gives this woman to be wed?' and the woman's hands are offered up by her father, or whoever is giving her away. The woman's hands are then placed in those of her partner. The wrists are crossed, with right hand clasping right hand and left hand clasping left hand. The ribbon is wound around their wrists. It is looped over the top of one and under and around the other. This never-ending loop represents infinity. A red cord or ribbon is usually used, as red symbolises the passion and vitality that flourishes between the couple. The tightness of the loop represents the length of time for which the couple will be bound together: a loose loop represents a year and a day whereas a tight loop represents a more permanent union. The modern expression 'tying the knot' is derived from this tradition. In olden days the priest or minister might enclose the clasped hands in his stole and perform the blessing. This was to symbolise the trinity of marriage: man and woman united by God.

Handfasting also has its own ritualistic divorce known as a handparting. Here the cord is tied at the beginning of the ceremony only to be severed at the end, representing the breakdown of the union.

Nowadays handfasting is often incorporated into ceremonies for different reasons; some couples simply find it romantic whilst others wish to honour an old tradition. Pagans and Wiccans regularly perform the ceremony, attracted by the fact that the custom is not weighed down by legal technicalities. The pledge the couple make is seen as embodying much stronger ties than any offered by a Church or State union. In modern times, when couples often choose to have a family and live together without taking the extra step up the wedding aisle, handfasting can be a nice alternative. It formalises a relationship in the eyes of family and friends and allows a couple to live together in a simple partnership that eliminates unnecessary third and fourth parties.

Chapter 6

The Dress

For many brides, choosing a wedding dress continues to be one of the most important parts – if not *the* most important part – of planning their wedding day. Some wedding guides even recommend starting with the dress and planning the rest of the day around it. In some ways this may make sense – a woman's choice of dress can be quite a good indication of her style in general.

Weddings seem to bring out the traditionalist within many women (and men), perhaps because weddings are still as much about continuity as they are about new beginnings. We all seem to be very concerned with 'personalising' our weddings and making them 'unique', but at the same time want to do things 'the way they always have been done'. Perhaps this explains why so many prospective brides still opt for white weddings, even if they are unconventional and non-traditional in other areas of their lives. Because the veiled figure in the white gown has become so fixed in our imaginations as the quintessential bride, we forget that the white wedding is quite a recent arrival on our shores.

The white dress is now a cosmopolitan fashion, worn by brides from Tokyo to Tipperary. It has become practically universal in these days of mass communication, thanks to images of 'princess brides' – from Victoria and Margaret to Grace and Diana – being beamed at us from royal weddings, and more recently from celebrity weddings. About two centuries ago, however, it would have been unthinkable for most Irish women to purchase such an impractical and expensive dress that could only be worn once. Today, buying a dress that a woman will probably only wear once is a grand gesture that is, for most of us, reserved for our wedding day. For generations of Irish women who came before us, it would have been reserved for day-dreams – if they even dreamt about such things at all.

For many of us today, getting married is one of the few opportunities we have to participate in ritual and ceremony. While other parts of our lives are no longer governed by strict social codes and elaborate etiquette, we still tend to feel that when we get married there are certain correct ways of doing things, and because many of us don't know these rules of social conduct or understand where they came from, we tend to look for guidance to the recent past, and so assume that The Big White Dress is the traditional wedding dress. We also feel a sense of connectedness with the women who went before us by following in their footsteps; we follow the rules they followed, we hang on to their superstitions, and we wear what they wore. Their wedding day is also one of the few days, for many women, when they are the focus of so much attention and scrutiny, so there is a lot of comfort to be had from knowing that you are doing things just as they always have been done – in recent times, anyway.

Due to this, and to the fact that the wedding dress has now become imbued with so much meaning for us – because it is such a grand gesture – dressing for one's wedding has become a very ritualized affair. Buying a wedding dress is one of the big 'markers' in a woman's life, and the fewer of these that we have (especially celebrated so publicly) the more important they become. This ritualization of dress, however, only really took place in the last 150 years. During this time, fashion has continued to affect the silhouette of the wedding dress, but not so much its colour or the most important accessory: the veil. Previously, however, fashion dictated what brides wore – as well as, of course, social restrictions, financial circumstances, and religious requirements.

In this chapter, we will be exploring just how traditional the white dress really is for Irish brides, and trying to uncover the origins and meaning behind various bridal accessories. While we strove for equality between the sexes, this just wasn't possible; there is far less information about men's wedding attire than there is about women's wedding wear. We apologise for this, and encourage any knowledgeable male readers to contact us with more information for any subsequent editions of this book.

We hope that, armed with a little more knowledge about how wedding fashions evolved, brides-to-be will be able to hit the shops with a more open mind or a clearer idea of what they want to get married in, and a sense of proportion regarding the importance of this decision. We would like to remind brides of the fact that traditions are started by individuals just like our dear readers – ordinary, normal people. Traditions evolve and change over time, to accommodate changing needs, priorities and lifestyles. If you choose to get married in a gown that does not, at first sight, seem traditional, this does not make your wedding any less authentic, or your vows less genuine. What may today seem like an 'alternative' way of celebrating your wedding could well be a revered and much-loved tradition for Irish brides 200 years from now.

We will begin by having a look at that defining feature of the modern wedding dress in western culture – its colour. Then we will take a tour through the various styles worn by brides over the centuries, giving examples of some of the lovely ladies who have gotten married in these styles, so they can be looked up for further inspiration by the reader. Before we go on, we would like to share some wise words from fashion editor Charles Worth that you might like to keep in mind as you search for your gown:

> A dress should never overpower the wearer. It should merely be an appropriate frame for a charming picture, bringing out the beauties of the picture, but never distracting attention from it.

The White Dress

The colour white has long been associated with weddings; Roman brides wore white 2,000 years ago, and many brides, from cultures all over the world, gravitate towards some shade of white today when dressing for their wedding day. Brides have, however, worn many other colours over the centuries. Ancient Hebrew brides are recorded as having worn blue; red was the traditional wedding colour in Europe during the Middle Ages – and still is in China, India, and many Islamic countries. In Norway green was the colour for weddings, while Icelandic brides wore black velvet with gold and silver threads. European royalty usually wore gold or silver, but white came back into fashion when Queen Victoria wore white for her wedding to Prince Albert in 1840.

Much has been made of the symbolic meaning of wearing white – the colour is often associated with purity and chastity. While Spenser did describe it, in the 1590s, as the colour 'that seemes a virgin best[11]', the 'rule' that only virgin brides are entitled to wear white at their weddings is a relatively recent social convention that would appear to have outlived its relevance at this point. Today, women who wear white do so because they associate the colour with weddings and with wedding joy, not because they wish to present themselves as paragons of virtue.

White has also been favoured by wealthy brides over the centuries because it is so impractical – to wear a dress in a costly white fabric (which is very difficult to keep clean) shows the world that the bride can afford to take great care of her appearance and that she can afford to purchase a dress that she may only wear once. The implication is that both the woman and the event she celebrates in this dress are very important. This is one of the reasons why we tend to wear white dresses today – we reserve the grand gesture of buying what for some of us will be the most expensive item of clothing we will ever own, and wear for one day only, for our weddings. Many of us have the luxury of not having to worry about being able to wear it again. During the 1800s in Ireland, white was popular among upper-class brides, but it was also the popular colour for 'full dress at parties'[12] and it is impossible to know which inspired which. In this century, inspired by Queen Victoria, the concept of the 'white wedding' began to develop, but before this, and for most women for a long time after Victoria's wedding, getting married simply meant wearing your Sunday best, whatever that might be.

Coloured bridal dresses were very common in Ireland. In the fifteenth century, one Irish bride is recorded as having worn a red tunic under a blue one on her wedding day, and in seventeenth-century Kildare another bride is remembered as having worn a red petticoat with green tape on the skirt and waistcoat and a handkerchief on her head. Up until the nineteenth century, colours favoured for wedding dresses changed like any other fashion. Even after Queen Victoria set the trend for wearing white, other colours continued to be worn, and they often had their own symbolic meaning:

> *Married in white, you have chosen right,*
> *Married in blue, your love will always be true,*
> *Married in pearl, you will live in a whirl,*
> *Married in brown, you will live in town,*
> *Married in red, you will wish yourself dead,*
> *Married in yellow, ashamed of your fellow,*
> *Married in green, ashamed to be seen,*
> *Married in pink, your spirit will sink,*
> *Married in grey, you will go far away,*
> *Married in black, you will wish yourself back.*

From Ballgowns to Mini-Skirts

Irish fashion is, arguably, only really coming into its own now. It has, for a very long time and for obvious reasons, largely followed British and continental fashions. Particularly during the eighteenth and nineteenth centuries, upper-class Irish brides would have worn quite similar wedding dresses to British brides. If the history of wedding dresses that follows seems to focus very much on British bridal fashions, this is why.

During the Regency period (1790-1825), a style called Empire line, originating in France, became popular in England. It is defined by a raised waistline that is cut just beneath the bust, with a skirt that drops to the floor from the hem, giving the wearer an elongated silhouette. According to designer Philip Delamore, this style of dress was historically often worn with a cropped bolero or Spencer Jacket in velvet or brocade, or with a wrap.[13] The Empire line dress was inspired by the Greco-Roman style of draped tunics that became popular during the Napoleonic Empire's spread across Europe towards the Middle East. The fashion was quite short-lived and symbolised a period of classical enlightenment and unrestrained dressing for women – if this style appeals to you, then for inspiration look no further than Jane Austen's heroines. The subsequent, heavily constructed and corseted clothing that became fashionable for the remainder of the nineteenth century restricted women's movement and was far less practical. If you would like to re-create this style, you need only decide if you want to go for the period look – with, say, an ostrich feather fan – or if you prefer the revival look, *à la* Holly Golightly, complete with opera-length gloves.

While Empire line gowns would have been fashionable among upper-class Irish brides, most Irish women would, at this time, have worn a suit for their weddings. These suits were not always brand new, and they would almost certainly have been expected to be worn again. Suits were very popular in a range of colours, particularly lilac and pale blue. In the 1850s browns and purples, in silk and with crinolines, were most popular, but frocks in blue and grey check, or oyster-coloured silk, were also recorded in the diaries of fashionable ladies as having been worn by brides. Brides often wore two-piece outfits because they could subsequently be matched with other garments more easily that way.

In the second half of the nineteenth century purples were also very popular, and velvet and other materials became more fashionable. The popularity of these shades seems to have had something to do with the fact that mourning appears to have been almost a national pastime in Britain at the time, so this colour was quite appropriate for a number of social occasions and soon became popular even with women who were not in mourning.

Towards the end of the century, gowns became more and more formal among those who could afford them, with court trains that descended all the way from the shoulder and were draped in Limerick lace. At this time, brides sometimes wore hats or bonnets with flowers and feathers, and they often accessorised with paisley shawls, which came to be known as bridal shawls.

The ballgown, which we have come to see as the archetypal wedding dress, worn by the romantic fairytale princess, dates from around this period at the end of the nineteenth century, when gowns became more restrictive and formal, with corsets and layers of petticoats and great big hoops to give fullness to the skirts. This type of gown has a fitted bodice and voluminous skirt, as well as a train. It was, and usually still is, worn with a veil. It is often one piece, but can also consist of two separate pieces.

As Philip Delamore explains in his book *The Wedding Dress*,

the Victorian era was pivotal in the development of fashion as an industry; this is the period in history when the dressmaker was transformed into the designer. A series of innovations and changes, such as the invention of the domestic sewing machine, the industrialisation of textile production for fabrics such as lace, and the establishment of the first couture houses in Paris created a consumer market for fashion to an aspirational nouveau riche, and a burgeoning middle class. Journalism and an opening up of international markets, particularly in the New World, saw illustrated journals describe in every detail every aspect of the court seasons and events, including numerous fashion plates and patterns, which could be recreated by the home dressmaker if a couturier was beyond your means.

It is easy to forget that this style was actually not far from the normal everyday dress of the period for most women, and wedding dresses were often altered to be worn again on other formal occasions. Queen Victoria herself did this, frequently wearing the lace overskirt from her wedding dress over other dresses. It is probably because we forget the origins of this style of wedding dress, and the context in which it became fashionable, that we overlook that it was a child of its time, and just one of many styles that women have adopted for their wedding attire.

This style is still a favourite, and if you are looking for more modern interpretations and inspiration there is plenty to choose from – from Elizabeth Taylor (for her first wedding) to Princess Diana, Mariah Carey and Victoria Beckham, many brides have opted for this style over the years.

Almost as popular as the ballgown and nearly as closely associated with brides is the princess line gown. Not so much a silhouette as a cut, this is a minimal and slimming style, characterised by vertical lines from the shoulder down to the hem. This style is attributed to Charles Worth who, as the nineteenth-century couturier for Princess Alexandra, created her dress for her wedding to Edward VII. Worth was an English designer, and he established the first couture house in Paris in 1858. He was responsible for many innovative styles adopted in the late nineteenth and early twentieth century.

Into the twentieth century, contemporary fashion continued to influence bridal fashions. During the first decade of the century, delicate gauze and silk creations were worn by fashionable ladies at weddings, and these were followed by the clothes of the Edwardian period, which were worn up until the outbreak of war. After the First World War, women's clothes allowed greater freedom of movement again, and were much more practical and less restrictive. Hemlines began to rise – in the 1920s short wedding dresses were almost universal. One style that emerged from this new, liberated approach to dressing women was the column dress, which was a slim, fitted style. Today column dresses can either be designed in an unconstructed 1920s flapper style, with a short skirt, or a long, lean style, typical of the 1950s.

These simple dresses, which emphasised freedom of movement, were again inspired by classical Greek and medieval dress (like Empire line dresses) and were in stark contrast to the Edwardian silhouette. The style represented freedom from the conventions of traditional fashion, and free spirits like the dancer and advocate of dress reform, Isadora Duncan, wore these dresses beautifully. This style became popular again in the 1960s and 1970s, and is quite popular with 'minimalist' brides today. This style would have been popular with the fashionable Irish bride too, because around this period wedding dresses in the British Isles often had a vaguely medieval character.

Again – many of these dresses were made to be worn on occasions other than just the wedding day, and fabrics like silk and georgette were very popular for these dresses. In the mid-1920s, some Irish brides favoured a dress and tunic combination, often embroidered and of woollen fabric, which in style echoed contemporary interpretations of Celtic Revivalism.[14] An Irish bride wanting to wear a Celtic-style gown today could look at relevant websites, listed at the end of this book, for inspiration.

The following decade, the 1930s, saw the beginning of the ritualization of dressing for one's wedding, but this development was interrupted by the Second World War and hampered by the fact that this ritual was not relevant to or obtainable for most Irish women at the time. In England and other parts of Britain, it was around this time that wedding attire started developing distinctive features that set it apart from the usual everyday wear. The silhouette that was popular at this time was the slender, elegant shape of movie stars clad in mermaid and fishtail gowns. The bias-cut gown of the 1930s Hollywood screen siren was the inspiration for these wedding gowns – it was a fluid alternative to the constructed column style. Once again, designers were inspired by classical Greek dress, and designer Madeleine Vionnet was a pioneer of bias-cutting. Her creations were worn by actresses like Marlene Dietrich, Joan Crawford and Katharine Hepburn. It was at this time that Hollywood began to challenge the couturiers in Paris for hegemony in the fashion world. Today, a cross-over between the slip dress (a relatively new item of outer-wear) and the mermaid or fishtail dress continues to be very popular with Irish brides.

The White Dress, in silk and lace, was starting to establish its status as *the* wedding dress at this point, but in Ireland it was not yet considered the quintessential wedding dress, and it had to wait for the end of the Second World War to really take a hold of women's collective imaginations and become 'every little girl's dream'. Though in many ways unaffected by the war, Ireland did have to contend with restrictions on many goods, including fabrics. As well as the scarcity of resources and money, there was a general feeling that it was not good to be seen indulging oneself and wasting money on big weddings, and war weddings were governed by the general austerity of the times. Except for women who had heirloom wedding dresses, or who managed to borrow a dress for the occasion from a friend, brides had to make do with what was available in times of rationing of fabrics and scarcity of bridal materials. The suit, a two-piece outfit consisting of a jacket and skirt – later trousers too – was the most popular and commonly seen wedding outfit during these years.

Suits were often brown in colour, sometimes trimmed with fur for a little luxury. Post-war, there was a return to more romantic dressing up, but many women continued to favour suits as an alternative to the white dress. The cultural revolution of the 1960s later saw the suit take on a new role – either overtly sexual (with a mini skirt or even hot pants), or androgynously blurring gender definitions. The rise in second and exclusively civil marriages has also been a part of the reason for the suit's enduring appeal, as it was seen by many women as being more appropriate than a white dress for such a wedding. For a really classy version of this look, see Marilyn Monroe at her wedding to Joe DiMaggio.

Other women were inspired by the images of princesses like Margaret in England and Grace in Monaco, in 1950s newspapers and magazines, to adopt the white dress with a veil again. While this typically can't be worn again, modern brides can often re-use their 'going away' outfit, which is produced and worn for leaving on honeymoon.

Gowns in the 1950s often featured beadwork like that seen on Princess Elizabeth's dress in 1947, and dresses became more voluminous again as rationing ended. The fashion at this time was actually for 'blush pink' rather than stark white – a subtle shade that was more flatting to pale British and Irish complexions. By the late 1950s, the 'tradition' of wearing a white dress was so well-established that the dress could be shortened without seeming too risqué, so long as it was still white. Some brides were still influenced by contemporary street fashion, daringly wearing pastels instead of white, and mid-calf bouffant dresses, sometimes of brocade or machine-made lace or other fabrics. The bouffant style maintained its popularity until the mid-1960s, when those who wanted to wear a short wedding dress usually chose a mini dress, again under the influence of contemporary street fashion. If this is a style that appeals to you, look to Mia Farrow, Cilla Black or Audrey Hepburn (second time around) for inspiration.

Another development of this era was the A-line silhouette, which also featured in wedding dresses. Closely related to the princess line cut, it was a child of the 1960s, with a simple fitted bodice and a flared skirt – basically a modern take on the classic ball-gown shape. It was worn both short and long, and emerged as a reaction to the unfeminine style that had been imposed by the war.

Some brides continued to choose to dress slightly more 'classically'; inspired by Sybil Connolly, they wore Irish wools and laces, and later on in the decade sheath-like Empire dresses were once again fashionable. This slim, elegant style remained popular throughout the 1970s and was then suddenly superseded by full, crinoline-skirted dresses again, probably inspired by the lavish and elaborate gown that Diana Spencer wore for her wedding to the Prince of Wales. That particular style won over a whole new generation of women, and was popular for a good decade, right through into the 1990s.

The '90s saw the rise of the 'themed' wedding, which has also had an impact on the choice of attire of brides and grooms. Couples who decide to have a *Lord of the Rings* wedding tend to dress in medieval-style clothes, while a bride who is inspired by art nouveau is more likely to wear a flapper-style dress, and so on. We have even heard rumours of Disney-themed wedding dresses, but this may just be an urban myth ...

Today, wedding fashions are still influenced by street fashion, but there is also a whole separate wedding fashion industry that follows its own rules and features completely different trends to the world of haute couture or high street fashion. As Linda May Ballard explains,

> Until quite recently, a wedding gown was usually a rather special version of contemporary fashion, rather than a distinctive and ritualized form of dress. While some brides may choose not to conform to this image, for many today the ideal is the "traditional" wedding gown, white and veiled.[15]

For many brides and designers alike, wedding dresses seem to be frozen at a certain point in time and have ceased to evolve along with every-day wear. Perhaps it is a reflection on our modern lives that we choose, in this arena, to hold on to styles that belong to another era, and that we hold this particular style up as *the* definitive bridal style that all women should aspire to and copy, regardless of how much we have changed in other regards in the intervening years.

Many Irish brides are beginning to be more confident about choosing alternative dresses, and with such a rich history of fashions, Irish women have many styles to choose from, even when they do want to be traditional. There are several young Irish designers who specialise in bridal wear, whose style is at times influenced by contemporary fashion and at other times completely innovative and original. Whether you would like a dress that is that little bit different, or exactly like the one your grandmother wore, you will almost certainly be able to find it somewhere on this island. From off-the-peg to made-to-measure, the possibilities are endless. At the back of this book we suggest a number of websites that you might like to have a look at when you search for The Dress. Before you head off in search of 'the one' or 'the one that will do', remember the old rhyme:

> *Something old, something new,*
> *Something borrowed, something blue,*
> *And a silver six-pence in her shoe.*

Something old, something new refers to the bride's passage from her old life to her new one – so wearing something old signifies continuity while wearing something new symbolises a new beginning. *Something borrowed* means that marriage involves sharing, *something blue* alludes to the colour's association with constancy, and *a silver sixpence in her shoe* refers to the hope of riches – in both a material and an emotional sense – in marriage. As long as you have all of these elements (on your person or in less tangible form), you'll have a beautiful day no matter which frock you choose to wear!

Finally, if you are at all superstitious, remember that it was believed to be bad luck for a bride to wear pearls on her wedding day (they are believed to resemble, and therefore symbolise, tears), and twentieth-century Irish brides believed that it was bad luck for the groom to see the bride before the ceremony on their wedding day.

Accessories

Much-loved by women, accessories are also very popular with the wedding industrial complex. This is one more area where salespeople will try to get you to part with substantial amounts of hard-earned cash. Many brides find themselves spending small fortunes on lace garters, for example, that they will never wear again, and the origins of which they may never discover.

So we will begin with this, somewhat controversial, accessory: the garter. While many brides now seem to think that it is worn simply so it can be removed – possibly with the groom's teeth – to the strains of a Tom Jones tune, its origins are actually even wilder. In medieval times it was believed that the bride's gown would bring others luck, so guests would tear a strip off the dress

to take home as a lucky talisman. Eventually, in order to avoid having their dresses torn to shreds by over-enthusiastic guests, brides took to tossing them a piece to fight over. This eventually evolved into the groom throwing the garter to his single friends. The lucky man who catches the garter is often treated to a dance with the lucky woman who catches the bouquet.

Which brings us to one of the best-loved bridal accessories in the west: the bouquet. Bouquets were originally just posies of fragrant herbs, carried to ward off evil spirits. In some European countries, brides also carried a sheaf of wheat to symbolise fertility. Brides in Northern Ireland often carried (and continue to carry) family bibles instead of bouquets up the aisle. Bouquets have gone from being small, compact posies (which the Victorians often carried in tussy mussies – little silver containers for the bouquet) to much larger arrangements, and back to being small and compact again. At different times they were carried in the crook of the arm or even in baskets, and the shape, size and composition of bridal bouquets have also varied at least as much as fashions for dresses have.

Another accessory that has been popular with some brides over the years is gloves. While not the most practical accessory (they have to be removed when the rings are exchanged and later to shake hands with guests), they do add a bit of old-style glamour to simple wedding gowns. In Ireland it was believed that gloves were an inappropriate gift for courting lovers to give each other, so that might explain why they weren't, and still aren't, hugely fashionable here. They were worn by a number of Irish brides in the nineteenth century, but were not particularly popular.

Even though many women seem to have something of a love affair with shoes, when you are getting married may not be the best time to invest in a new pair. According to Irish folklore, it was good luck to wear old shoes to one's wedding. New shoes might attract fairies, who would spirit the bride (or groom) away just to get their hands on the lovely footwear. It was also, as we have

already seen, considered good luck to get married in something old (old, new, borrowed and blue seem to keep popping up in different countries through the ages, in various guises), and shoes were a good option. New shoes would also have been quite expensive for the average couple in the nineteenth century, so this was a useful superstition for saving a bit of money. Finally, on a lighter note, leather also symbolised fertility, so some couples used to have an old pair of shoes thrown over them when they left the church, for good luck.

'Princess for a Day'

While headdresses – from tiaras to veils – are, strictly speaking, accessories, they are so important to many brides that they deserve to have a section devoted exclusively to them.

Today, brides often wear a tiara for its associations with royalty, because they want to be 'a princess for a day', but wearing a tiara also has connotations of Adam and Eve, the king and queen of creation, according to Philip Delamore's brilliant *The Dress: A Sourcebook*. In some Scandinavian and Russian Orthodox ceremonies, a crown is still placed on the bride's head during the ceremony. If you have an heirloom tiara to wear, this may be an option for you. Alternatively, you could buy or make one, as there is a huge selection of models and materials available. Some brides, inspired by the Celts, are opting to wear minns, and for more information about minns please see Chapter 7.

Other possible headdresses include flowers, headbands, hats, caps, feathers, and veils. Women have always used flowers to adorn themselves, and certain flowers are particularly strongly associated with brides, like orange blossoms. They were very popular with Roman brides, and the custom of wearing them was revived by Queen Victoria, who wore a garland of orange blossoms at her wedding. One story that explains why brides wear orange blossoms goes back to French lore, which has it that orange blossoms became a symbol of good fortune following a deal made between a Spanish girl and a French nobleman. The nobleman wanted a clipping from an orange tree that he had seen in the garden of the king of Spain. When the king refused him, he paid a poor gardener's daughter to get him a clipping. The young woman used this money as a dowry so that she could marry her lover, which she would otherwise not have been able to afford to do. Because she was so grateful, and to honour her benefactor, the girl wore orange blossoms in her hair on her wedding day, and so a tradition was begun. The floral chaplet was made popular again in the 1980s, often quite oversized and in Fairy Queen styles. The twentieth century also saw brides wearing the 'Miner's lamp' at various times: a large single flower that is worn at the front of the head like a miner's lamp, which is where it gets its name.

The veil is the accessory that is most closely associated with brides – many of the other accessories can be worn by women at other times, but this one immediately identifies a woman as a bride.

Between the early nineteenth and the mid-twentieth centuries, more was contributed to the ritualized appearance of the bride by her veil than by her gown. Although her dress was often stylish enough to be obviously 'bridal', it could also be worn on other occasions, and in style it bore a close relationship to everyday dress. While fashion may often have attempted to dictate otherwise, brides have long chosen to veil their faces for their wedding ceremonies.[16]

In times of arranged marriages, when the bride and groom did not see each other until they were wed, the purpose of the veil was to conceal the face of the bride until she reached the altar or until a particular point in the ceremony. In this tradition, the lifting of the veil signified a woman's passage from her father's home to her husband's. The veil seems to have been introduced into Europe from the Middle East, brought back by knights from the Crusades. In the arranged marriages of the time, the veil was used to hide the bride's face from the groom, who would not hitherto have seen her. Once they were married the groom could unveil his wife's face, as it was too late for second thoughts then. This may be the reasoning behind the Jewish tradition of the groom checking to see if the bride is the girl of his choosing before he places the veil over her head.

At times the veil has also been considered an important form of protection from evil for the bride. Ancient Roman brides wore red veils to defy demons, or yellow veils known as *flammeum*, dyed with saffron to represent the flame of Vesta, the domestic goddess and giver of life. Because the veil obscured the face of the bride, it was thought that evil spirits would be confused and leave her unmolested.

Fashions for wearing veils came and went and changed with the times, and it was the Victorians again who really cemented the fashion for veils. Victorian brides wore a veil to symbolise modesty, respect and virginity. Irish brides didn't always take the veil off immediately after the ceremony, and sometimes it still covered their faces as they left the church. Limerick lace seems to have been a popular fabric for veils among Irish brides.

At the beginning of the twentieth century, many brides favoured the 'motoring' veil, a very short veil that envelops only the face. It was a practical choice for daring, modern brides who travelled to their wedding by bicycle. In the 1920s, brides who wore a veil usually wore it anchored low on the forehead. This fashion began just after the end of the First World War and became increasingly popular from that point onwards.

Subsequently, hats became the fashionable headdress for brides, but sometimes hats were worn with veils – so important was it for brides to incorporate a veil in their bridal outfit. In the middle of the twentieth century, when hemlines rose, short, bouffant veils that echoed the shape of dresses became fashionable. Today, with a wedding industry that has its own fashions, it is possible for a bride who wants to wear a veil to choose one that is any length, in almost any fabric or colour – the only limit is her imagination.

If you are about to begin searching for your wedding attire, please keep a few things in mind. You will probably end up choosing a different style to the one you have in mind when you set out – most women do. Keep an open mind and bring a friend whose opinion you value. If you can't find what you are looking for, consider a dressmaker. You must have complete confidence in him or her though! Also try vintage shops and eBay – but be careful and always get references. Above all, have fun – and keep your priorities in perspective ... Perhaps the Goldsmiths both got it half-right:

> I chose my wife, as she did her wedding gown, for qualities that would wear well.
>
> — Oliver Goldsmith, *c.*1769

The Groom

There have been many changes in what men have worn on their wedding day – mostly because there have been changes in men's fashions. Generally speaking, men simply wore more formal and better-quality versions of what they would have worn every day when dressing for their weddings. Some grooms wore a top hat and tails, but many wore drab and unremarkable lounge suits, as Linda May Ballard puts it in *Forgetting Frolic*. In the twentieth century, grey 'morning suits' were often preferred to the usual black suits. Today, grooms have a large variety of suits to choose from, and often incorporate the 'signature colour' of the wedding in their attire. We have been unable to find an exclusively wedding-related outfit or special, historical wedding accessory for the Irish groom, but welcome hearing from attentive readers who will be able to point out to us what we have overlooked.

Chapter 7

Planning an Irish Wedding: From Betrothal to the Flowers of the Home

Marriage is a ritual that has been celebrated in our culture for centuries. When couples decide to get married, a world of traditions, customs and superstitions is often revealed to them – for better or for worse. Some couples will try to keep their weddings as 'modern' as possible, while others will take the opportunity to learn more about their culture's wedding traditions. This chapter will take the more curious readers on a journey through wedding planning and celebrations in Ireland over the centuries, sometimes suggesting how an old tradition might be updated or incorporated into a more modern wedding.

You will find here ideas and anecdotes related to clothes, invitations, vows, food, music and other wedding-related subjects. This is not, however, a guide to organising your wedding, and should not be used as such. We have not included time-lines or to-do lists with boxes to tick. For these sorts of things, please have a look at the Useful Websites section, where we list sites that supply very good planning tools.

We have tried to steer clear of leprechauns and fairy wings for flower girls – there is enough of that out there already, and if that is the sort of wedding you would like to have, then this is not the book for you. While it is not for any one individual to be the arbiter of what is uniquely and authentically Irish, we do feel that it is important not to mix and match traditions too freely if they are to retain any of the value that we attach to them because they are *Irish* traditions. So if you would like to have bagpipes, for example, at your wedding, by all means have them – but bear in mind that they are Scottish, not Irish.

Butter and Burials

Obviously the first step towards having an Irish wedding – or any kind of wedding, for that matter – is to get engaged. There are a few uniquely Irish ways of getting engaged, more of which below. Before we come to that, however, we would just like to state an obvious fact that can sometimes be overlooked in the excitement and the hype created around the whole issue: the proposal is not that important. Yes, most women would be very pleased to get one of those supremely romantic proposals on top of the Eiffel Tower or on a gorgeous tropical beach. Most women would not say no to having a trail of rose petals strewn about the house leading them to a little blue box from Tiffany's. But for many couples, it just doesn't work out like that. And that's fine – because you will hopefully both be so thrilled to be marrying each other that the specifics of the proposal really won't matter that much. And there is no evidence to suggest that a magnificent proposal makes for a happier marriage, so if you (or your fiancée) are not the types for dramatic romantic surprises, take heart!

If you would like to propose to your girlfriend the (very) old-fashioned way, why not take your beloved to a stream, present her with a little pot of newly-churned butter and recite this old saying:

Oh woman, loved by me, mayest thou
give me thy heart, thy soul and body.

It might be an idea to bring a picnic so that you can then put the butter to some more practical use. The idea behind bringing the butter would seem to have been that it symbolised the wealth and abundance that the man hoped for in his marriage, as butter was a luxury in rural Ireland in centuries past.

If you are fairly certain that your prospective fiancée has a good sense of humour, you may also like to try asking her, 'Would you like to be buried with my people?' or 'Would you like to hang your washing next to mine?'. The former originates from the custom of burying women with their husbands' families instead of their own, and of course the latter implies that you would like to live with your intended – but not in sin.

A final word of warning to the eager groom-to-be: unless you are absolutely certain that your intended will feel comfortable with this, do not propose in a public setting. Even if she is thrilled to get engaged to you, she may not want everyone else on the Eiffel Tower to share the moment.

If you are a lady and tired of waiting for him to propose, seize the moment when the next leap-year comes around and propose to him yourself. The ring is optional – at least as far as the authors could ascertain, but the etiquette on that could change quite quickly, so do double-check before proposing.

With this Ring ...

Whether you decide to have an engagement ring or not, you probably will have wedding bands, so below are a few ideas for both.

The tradition of the groom proposing to his bride-to-be with an engagement ring began in AD860, when Pope Nicholas I decreed that a groom had to present his intended with a gold ring in order to prove that his intentions were honourable and genuine. Diamonds were made fashionable by King Maximilian of Hapsburg, who gave Mary of Burgundo a diamond engagement ring in 1477. The special significance of diamonds is that they are fairly indestructible, so it is hoped that the feelings of the couple will, like the ring, last for all eternity. If you prefer a different stone, you can also choose to get a ring with your birthstone, or some other stone that you are fond of.

To many couples, the rings are very important, and they give a lot of thought to them. This is probably because they will (hopefully) be wearing them for the rest of their lives, so they want to make sure that they will like them. More importantly though, the rings are a couple's public and outward sign of commitment. Wearing this ring on the fourth finger of your left hand expresses to the world that you are in a relationship and have made a permanent commitment. It was once believed in Ireland that wedding rings were worn on the fourth finger of the left hand because the blood line in this finger went directly to the heart. This belief probably comes from the Romans, who in turn most likely adopted it from the Egyptians. In some European countries, the engagement ring is worn on the fourth finger of the right hand, instead of the left hand. Some women choose not to wear an engagement ring at all, though for some reason this seems to be frowned upon. We suspect it may be the diamond industry doing most of the frowning, though.

Unlike diamond engagement rings, which are relatively new, as we saw above, wedding rings go back to the earliest days of civilisation, when the betrothal ritual – getting engaged – involved an exchange of property between the groom-to-be and the bride's parents. This was an important part of the marriage contract because the bride's family was losing her to another family, to another line. The gold ring was a sort of compensation for the bride's family and dates back to a time when gold rings were circulated as currency. Gold rings were so important in eighteenth-century Ireland that poor couples would go so far as to rent rings for their ceremony. Couples who could not afford a gold ring were even known to use the loop of the door key to their new home or to the church as symbolic rings.

As mentioned above, if you prefer other stones, an engagement ring doesn't need to have a diamond. It could also feature the bride-to-be's birth stone:

Month	Birthstone	Meaning
January	Garnet	Constancy
February	Amethyst	Sincerity
March	Aquamarine	Courage
April	Diamond	Innocence
May	Emerald	Success
June	Pearl	Health
July	Ruby	Contentment
August	Peridot	Happiness
September	Sapphire	Wisdom
October	Opal	Hope
November	Topaz	Fidelity
December	Turquoise	Prosperity

As for uniquely Irish wedding rings, there are a few other ideas you might consider. Do keep in mind though that despite their Irish or Celtic origins, the following are not actually commonly used in Ireland now, and are probably most popular with Americans of Irish descent.

The Claddagh ring continues to be a popular choice, and there is a great variety of modern and updated designs to choose from now. For a history of the Claddagh ring, please see Chapter 4.

You could also use a Celtic wedding ring – a ring with a design that is Celtic-inspired. It's hard to tell now exactly what all the different designs symbolised, so you can really use your imagination and get creative here. There is a design that has come to be known as the Celtic Love Knot, so-called because it is a pattern that is created by using continuous unending lines, symbolising eternity, unity and fidelity. You might also consider incorporating an animal in the design, like the heron, which mates for life. If you intend to use such a ring as your wedding band, you may want to have it made especially by a goldsmith. For inspiration, have a look at some of the early illuminated gospels, like the *Book of Kells*, which is full of beautiful designs that could be incorporated on your rings.

You could also make your wedding band a little different by incorporating a gemstone in it, such as an emerald. This tends to be used by couples of Irish descent because the colour green is associated with Ireland, but keep in mind that it is considered a most magical stone by forest spirits and Irish fairies. Great care should be taken when a bride wears an emerald, or she could be spirited away by the little people. (It is also considered unlucky for the bride to wear green on her wedding day, so if she is at all superstitious, she should steer clear of those gorgeous Vera Wang creations with the green velvet sashes).

Finally, there is also the Gimmal Ring – this is one ring that joins with another to complete an image, so that one could be given as an engagement ring, and the second as a wedding band, making it complete. In medieval times these rings, often in three parts rather than just two, were used as a promise of betrothal. One of each of the three parts of the ring was kept respectively by the girl, her suitor, and the priest. The three were reunited at the marriage ceremony and were worn by the bride as her wedding ring. Gimmal rings often look like the Claddagh ring – usually the ring's design is two hands that surround and cover a hidden heart or hearts. More modern Gimmal rings are usually made as one unit, with the hands hinged. When opened, the hands expose the heart that is hidden underneath. Again, very few Irish couples would opt for this, but if it feels right and you like the way it looks, you could certainly use one of these rings.

Finally, before you set off to buy the ring, remember that Irish lore warns that a bride should not shop for a wedding band on a Friday.

Let the Planning begin ...

Once you are engaged you are likely to want to tell the world all about it. Before you do, though, it might be an idea to sit down together and decide what kind of wedding you would like to have, and to make sure that you have a clear idea of what you both want before you start to plan (and shop).

Also – a word on themed weddings, since they are becoming so very popular. Like any other party, a wedding doesn't really need a theme – if anything, it already has one: marriage. But themes can sometimes make parties more enjoyable than they might otherwise have been, so if you are into themes, by all means choose one. If you are of Irish extraction and would like to express this during your wedding that's perfectly lovely, but we would advise you not to take the 'theme' too far. So if you would like to have an Irish wedding then your background and heritage would obviously inform your choices, but perhaps not be a theme in itself because, before you know it, it could turn into a Paddy's Day theme park, which is probably not the look you are aiming for on your wedding day.

Be prepared for everyone to have an opinion on everything about your wedding – sometimes quite strong opinions too! Books, magazines and wedding websites are very useful places for finding information, and online wedding forums are great for getting feedback on ideas you have, but remember that if you post a message asking for opinions, well ... it's the internet. You will find many very helpful people out there, but also many very angry, bitter and nasty people, just like in real life. Weddings are emotional and intensely personal events, as well as social occasions, so they bring out strange things in people. Learn to choose your battles and try to avoid being a Bridezilla when it comes to decisions big and small. Which takes us to the first really big decision you have to make: setting the date.

Setting the Date

It's unlucky to change the wedding date once it's set, so choose carefully! You may want to choose the date first if there is a particular one that means something to you, or you may want to check the availability of your chosen venues (for churches and hotels/castles, and so on) first and work around that.

If you are getting married in Ireland be realistic about the weather, and make sure you are prepared for all eventualities. If it's important to you to have a sunny day, try putting a statue of the Child of Prague in the garden the night before and say a little prayer, or consider getting married abroad. And remember that in Italy they say '*sposa bagnata, sposa fortunata*' (which translates roughly as 'lucky the bride who is rained upon'), and in many parts of Asia rain on your wedding day is considered a special blessing, so you really can't lose.

Try to choose a date that will not only suit you but all of the people you would like to have at the wedding to celebrate with you. People will make an effort, but remember that your day is not nearly as important to everyone else as it is to you, so be considerate. If you choose a popular day, month, or venue, start organising and booking early. The most popular day is Saturday, and the most popular months are May and June.

So to work from the more general to the specific, let's have a look at the times of year during which the Irish have traditionally married.

Beltaine

This festival, which starts around 1 May, celebrates fertility and new life and used to mark the beginning of summer in the old Irish calendar. The word is thought to mean 'brilliant fire' or 'new fire'. It was believed that this was a time for betrothal between Celtic gods and goddesses, so it was understandably popular among mortals. If you get married around this time you might like to have a bonfire, if practical (and safe – consult your venue before you start stacking the firewood), to make like the Celts who used to dance around fires at this time of year. If that's a little too wild for

you, you might just want to have an evening wedding with lots of candles and a roaring fire in the fireplace at your reception venue.

You could also have a May bush, since this was another custom that the Celts would have practiced around this time of year. The bride and groom would be presented with a May bush, and everyone would dance around it. If you don't want to do the dancing part, perhaps you could just use it as decor.

Lughnasa

This festival in early August celebrates the first day of autumn and the beginning of the harvest. Many historians believe that this was one of the most popular times for marriage among the Celts, as it was thought to be a good idea for young men to take a wife to see them through the long, cold winter. A place that was particularly popular during Lughnasa in the seventeenth century was Teltown, County Meath, where 'Teltown marriages' took place. They were performed in a place known as the 'marriage hollow' because the men and women who participated in the ceremony often held hands through a holed stone.

Because Lughnasa celebrated the imminent harvest, there would be great feasts at which people would eat the last of their stored food or the first of the harvest. One way of including this could be to serve locally harvested produce at your reception – the first of the wild berries become available at this time of year, for example, so you could use them in your dessert or wedding cake.

Samhain

This takes place between late October and early November. It means 'November' in Irish and also means, more generally, that summer has come to an end and that we are entering the twilight period of winter.

Back in the day, the storytelling would start around this time each year, and in many chieftains' halls a story had to be told every night during the winter months. If you think your guests would be inclined to cooperate you could ask them to tell stories at your wedding, and once they get a few drinks into them, experience shows that they may actually just do it of their own accord without having to be asked.

If you are considering getting married around Lughnasa or Samhain do keep in mind that while this was a favourite time for getting married in the ninth century, most likely because the summer harvest was completed and people had more food and wealth in the fall than at any other time of the year, as mentioned above, there are other reasons for *not* getting married at this time of year – in the nineteenth century it was believed that those who married in autumn would die the following spring, according to Lady Wilde.

In spite of this, November was popular during the early twentieth century, and a rhyme from Clare Island explains why:

November is said time to wed.
The crops is made and no warmth in bed!

Imbolc

This is celebrated around 1 February, on what was considered the first day of spring in the Celtic calendar. Just like at Beltaine, ceremonial fires would be lit to celebrate the awakening of the earth and the new life that would start in this season. It seems quite appropriate to get married during Imbolc in order to celebrate the new life that the bride and groom will share.

Other times that used to be considered appropriate for getting married include Shrove Tuesday, the last Tuesday before Lent, because it was the last opportunity to have a big feast before Lent. It is also sometimes called Pancake Tuesday because people would use up the last of the dairy and eggs in their pantry before Lent and make pancakes, and you could discuss with your caterer if they could incorporate this into the menu somehow.

There are other favourable days to marry, according to Irish tradition. Christmas and New Year's Day are considered lucky days to tie the knot, as is St Patrick's Day (but beware of turning it into a Leprechaun extravaganza. The last day of the old year is also considered especially lucky for weddings; it is thought that your last memories of the year you marry in should be the happiest ones.

If all of the information above is a little bewildering, perhaps this rhyme will simplify things for you:

> *Married when the year is new, he'll be loving, kind and true.*
> *When February birds do mate, you wed nor dread your fate.*
> *If you wed when March winds blow, joy and sorrow both you'll know.*
> *Marry in April when you can, joy for maiden and for man.*
> *Marry in the month of May, and you'll surely rue the day.*

Marry when June roses grow, over land and sea you'll go.
Those who in July do wed, must labour for their daily bread.
Whoever wed in August be, many a change is sure to see.
Marry in September's shrine, your living will be rich and fine.
If in October you do marry, love will come but riches tarry.
If you wed in bleak November, only joys will come, remember.
When December snows fall fast, marry and true love will last.

And when you're narrowing it down remember:

Marry on Monday for health,
Tuesday for wealth,
Wednesday the best day of all,
Thursday for losses,
Friday for crosses,
Saturday no luck at all.

And finally, it was said to be lucky if you married during a growing moon and a flowing tide, so you might like to get out your *Farmer's Almanac* before you settle on a date.

The Bridal Party

Once you have chosen a date, you might want to start thinking about the bridal party. The custom of having bridesmaids originated with the notion that there might be evil sprits at the wedding who would want to either harm the bride or spirit her away (think little people here). By dressing a number of young women similarly, it was hoped that the spirits would be confused and would not bother harming all of the young ladies present. This may be where the custom of dressing bridesmaids alike has come from, but since the bride is usually dressed very differently from her bridesmaids nowadays, that really isn't going to do anything for her in terms of keeping the spirits at bay. Most brides nowadays seem to do this because they like the way it looks.

Speaking of looks – if you are dictating what your bridesmaids must look like on the day, you may well be expected to pay for them to look this way. Whether or not you pay for their dresses is entirely up to you, but if you are not paying then you have to take into consideration what they can afford and whether or not they can wear their outfits again when you choose their dresses. The same applies to hair and makeup – if they are required to look a certain way, the bride needs to organise this and pay for it. Asking bridesmaids to cut their hair, hide tattoos, apply fake tan or lose weight is out of the question, no matter who pays for what. This sort of thing is venturing into Bridezilla territory and has been known to sour many a friendship.

When selecting bridesmaids, the bride should keep in mind that it was once considered unlucky for a woman to be a bridesmaid more than twice – 'three times a bridesmaid, never a bride'. This saying may come in handy when trying to decide who to ask to be a bridesmaid, as this can be quite tricky. It is perfectly acceptable to have only one bridesmaid or maid of honour, or to have ten if you are so inclined. Once you go over three it does tend to look a little over the top, but it all depends on the size and level of formality of your wedding. Don't feel pressured into asking people you don't want to – either because you aren't close to them, don't think they would do a good job, or because you already have enough bridesmaids, thank you very much. Most women will be quite understanding and may even be grateful not to be asked – being a bridesmaid can be quite costly and time-consuming.

It still is today, and has been for some time, customary for the groom (or the bride and groom) to give their bridesmaids a gift as a sign of their appreciation and to express their gratitude for the bridesmaids' support and friendship. Often, the bride and groom have much to be grateful for, as the bridesmaids will have been helping them to organise things behind the scenes for months before the wedding. This gift used to be jewellery, and quite detailed descriptions of such gifts could be found in *The Irish Times* in the 1920s and 1930s. Today, this sort of thing tends not to make it into the papers anymore, and all sorts of gifts are acceptable, from perfumes to pashminas to simple necklaces.

So what does a bridesmaid do?

- She helps choose the bride's dress and any other dresses that are needed, like the bridesmaids' dresses and dresses for the flower girls and ring bearers, if applicable.
- She organises the hen party for the bride. This is a relatively new concept in Irish pre-wedding parties, and has gone from being a gathering to wish the future bride good luck, to being a night (or even a whole week) of drunken debauchery. Because this is essentially a party that celebrates the bride, she shouldn't really organise it herself or dictate how it should be run. She is, however, strongly encouraged to voice any reservations about strippers and embarrassing gifts, jokes and games if she is worried that her bridesmaid might go down this road.
- She attends the wedding rehearsal so that she is clear on who stands where and does what, when.
- She may stay with the bride on the night before the wedding for moral support.
- She helps the bride to get ready on her wedding day.

- She is waiting at the church when the bride arrives and makes sure all is in order: makeup, hair, veil, train, etc.
- She keeps an eye on the flower girls and page boys, if there are any.
- She holds the bride's bouquet during the ceremony.
- She stands with the bride and groom during the vows.
- She signs the register as an official witness – unless you would like to have someone else do this.
- She accompanies the best man up the aisle.
- She makes a speech at the reception if she wants to.
- She helps the bride to take off her veil and fix her hair and makeup after the ceremony.

The groom, of course, also needs to choose an honour attendant or two. All the groom really needs, like the bride, are two people who stand up with him and act as witnesses. He may, however, choose to have a number of groomsmen, who all help the best man out with his duties. The custom of having a best man originated in times when brides were actually abducted by their grooms, and the best man would help the groom to fend off any of the bride's family trying to retrieve her.

The best man:

- helps the groom to choose his suit and any others that are needed.
- organises the stag party – which has in recent times mutated into week-long drinking sessions in Eastern Europe for some fortunate grooms.
- attends the rehearsal.
- gets the groom to the church on time.

- collects money from the bride and groom to pay ceremony fees and any suppliers who need to be paid on the day.
- keeps an eye on groomsmen and ushers.
- stands with the bride and groom during vows.
- takes care of the rings and produces them at the appropriate moment.
- makes sure everyone gets from the church to the reception
- acts as toastmaster.
- dances with the maid of honour.
- takes charge of cards or gifts that guests bring to the reception.
- takes charge of the groom's suit after the wedding.
- ensures everything runs smoothly at the reception.

You can also have flower girls, (they are usually aged between three and eight), while boys can be page boys or ring bearers. They don't actually have much of a function beyond looking cute and carrying flowers and a ring pillow (that doesn't usually have the real rings on it).

As for the parents, in the past they would often have chosen their child's future spouse, so would have been quite heavily involved in the wedding preparations. Today, the mother of the bride will still often help the bride to organise the wedding, and most of the planning tends to be done by the bride's family. This is probably a result of the fact that the bride's family used to pay for most of the wedding. The father of the bride doesn't usually pay for the whole wedding anymore, but he still tends to walk the bride down the aisle and 'give her away'. Nowadays, many brides choose to have both parents give them away, as they feel that this makes the giving away feel less like they are property that is being passed from one man to another, and more like they are leaving their family of origin and forming a new family with their partner.

Finally, a quick word on mothers-in-law. Your in-laws will most likely be a part of your life from now on. It is in everyone's best interest to have as good a relationship as possible, so it can be a good idea to include your future mother-in-law in the planning. It can give you a chance to get to know each other better and it will help her to feel included.

He who pays the piper ... Who pays for what?

We have outlined below what is considered to be the 'traditional' break-down of costs:

Bride's parents

- invitations
- other stationery
- bridesmaids' dresses
- wedding reception
- cake
- photographer
- music for ceremony
- flowers for the wedding venue
- bride's trousseau
- transport for bride and bridesmaids

Groom

- bride's engagement ring and wedding rings
- bride's and bridesmaids' bouquets
- suit hire for the groom, best man and groomsmen
- gifts for bridesmaids
- church fees
- honeymoon

That said – couples nowadays are generally expected to be able to pay for their own weddings, especially considering that they are often marrying later in life and living at home for longer, so they can save more money. The breakdown detailed above (compiled from a selection of wedding magazines, wedding websites and wedding books) can't be so very traditional anyway – having a photographer at your wedding is relatively new, so it's hardly 'traditional' for the bride's family to pay for this. Whatever the case, we would advise couples to clarify these things immediately to save themselves a lot of heartache and strife later on. Also remember that if you want to retain total control over how the money is spent you can only really do this if it's your own money. If you can't afford the wedding you want then you should wait and save more money or scale down. Do remember – it is your day, but it's also a big day for your families, and there are few things less attractive than a highly-strung young lady in a white dress throwing a fit over not having 'her' day go exactly to plan.

Location, location, location

When you decide what kind of wedding you want to have, one of the first decisions you have to make is whether or not you want a religious ceremony. We would recommend that you don't have your wedding in a church or other place of worship unless it really means something to at least one of you. That said, it's a private decision and you needn't feel like you have to justify your choice to anyone. As long as your officiant is happy to marry you and you both feel comfortable, you should celebrate your wedding in whatever way you choose.

Historically, Irish couples have tended to get married in the church they belonged to, though getting married at home was also in vogue for a time. The reception was usually held at the home of either the bride or groom's family, but this is not really an option for many people nowadays. There is a huge range of possible locations for wedding receptions, depending on your budget and priorities. Keep in mind that hospitality has traditionally been very important to the Irish, so the comfort of your guests – young and old – should be an important consideration. For useful resources for finding a venue, please see the Useful Websites section at the back of this book.

Pre-wedding Parties

Once the major decisions and down payments have been made, the pre-wedding parties can begin. Besides the infamous hen and stag parties, there are a few quainter ways of celebrating and preparing for the impending nuptials.

The ancient Brehon laws stated that before a man and woman could wed, the groom had to offer up 'tinnscra', or bride-price, to the father of the bride. It was believed that each person had a value and that when a bride was taken from her family, her value had to be compensated. This could be paid with cattle, land, horses, or gold and silver. This continued until well into the twentieth century, when matchmakers were in business all over Ireland. If you wanted to incorporate this it could be done with the two families sometime before the wedding, with the groom offering an old Irish coin (preferably not a Euro, the symbolism might be lost a little) to the bride's family. A word of warning to grooms-to-be though: many modern Irish brides may not find this terribly amusing.

While it is not new to celebrate the bride and groom passing from their single life to their married life by having a pre-wedding party of some description, the hen and stag nights that we have in Ireland today are fairly modern inventions. Before, family and friends of the bride would have a get-together in someone's kitchen, either to collectively make a quilt for the bride's bottom drawer, or to shower her with useful gifts for the kitchen. The bottom drawer of the nineteenth-century bride-to-be would have included household linens, including a christening robe and winding sheet for laying out a body, and a patchwork quilt. Sewing and lining a patchwork quilt for the bride was a communal activity, and a way for the female members of the community to shower the bride with their good wishes as well as giving her something practical that would last her a long time and be a constant reminder of her friends and family. Today, this still survives in some parts of Europe and the USA, where women have bridal showers as well as hen and stag nights.

Cork women sometimes still have a 'kitchen party' thrown for them, which all the female relations from both families, as well as friends, attend. Guests bring gifts for the couple's kitchen, and the bride-to-be is blindfolded and made to guess what each (wrapped) present is and who it's from.[17] This was much appreciated by brides who wouldn't have had anything for their kitchens because they were marrying straight out of their parents' homes.

If you wanted to do something similar today, you could get your friends to get together and make a ring bearer's pillow out of bits of fabric that mean something to them, to give you a sort of bottom drawer full of your friends' memories too. Or, if you have the time, and friends who can actually sew properly, you could even get them together to make you a quilt. You could also have a kitchen party rather than a hen night, and give it a modern twist and a slightly more adventurous theme: think 'stock the bar' parties, or a party where you are given exotic or luxury foods to stock your kitchen with, instead of appliances.

Another custom, already mentioned in Chapter 1, that could be revived today is that of inviting the groom to the bride's house right before the wedding and cooking a goose in his honour. Called 'eating the gander', it may be the origin of the old expression 'his goose is cooked' ...

Then there are, of course, those inescapable parties that most Irish brides and grooms are subjected/treated to today: the hen and stag night. Both the future groom and his bride will have one or more parties thrown for them that involve going out and getting very drunk, dressing up and doing fairly stupid things. Large quantities of alcohol tend to be consumed, and the groom-to-be will not infrequently find himself tied to a lamppost or naked on the pier in Dún Laoghaire the next morning. Increasingly, the bridesmaids and best men who organise these events are getting very ambitious and organising whole weekends, sometimes even weeks, away. Others are having more demure and civlised celebrations, like a day at a spa, a day out, or just a meal at someone's house. The important thing, really, is to make sure everyone can afford to come and that everyone involved, especially the bride- and groom-to-be, are comfortable with what goes on. No matter how they are celebrated, the idea behind these parties is to see the bride- and groom-to-be off, to have one last big party with their friends, and to help them prepare for marriage, be it materially (by making a quilt or giving them other useful gifts) or psychologically, by joining them for a last hurrah and goodbye to single life.

Finding 'The One'

No, we don't mean your future spouse. For many brides, their wedding dress is one of the most important aspects of the wedding. There are many traditions and superstitions that can be followed here to give this part of the preparations an Irish flavour.

If you would like to incorporate just a touch of Irish tradition in your wedding outfit, you could have a look at Tara brooches. The Celts had a great love of decorative ornamentation, and many beautifully crafted gold and silver pieces have survived and can be seen in museums today, including rings, bracelets, necklets, and ornamental brooches. One of the most famous of these is the Tara Brooch, used to fasten garments. It has been widely reproduced and shouldn't be too hard to find, and can be used discreetly on a coat or on the bouquet. You could have a look at displays in the National Museum, and some of the original jewellery might inspire you to purchase a similar item in one of the many gift shops that sell reproduction jewellery.

Another little detail that you could incorporate is a horseshoe, which is carried for good luck because 'horses were in the stall when Christ was born, and were blessed forevermore'. Instead of carrying a real horseshoe, you can now purchase small porcelain or crystal ones that can be discreetly attached to bouquets or pinned to dresses. Make sure that wherever you attach your horseshoe, the points are facing up so that your luck does not run out.

As mentioned above, the colour green, while associated with Ireland, is not thought to be lucky when it comes to weddings. It attracts the little people, and using too much of it may tempt them to spirit the bride away, so it is not recommended that the bride wears anything green.

As for the actual dress, if you would like to dress like the Irish brides that came before you, you have quite a lot of choice. Just like everywhere else, bridal fashions have come and gone in Ireland. For centuries, men and women have worn their best clothes on their wedding day. To buy or make a dress or suit that could not be worn again would have been considered foolish and wasteful in most societies, so wedding attire would generally have been very like everyday attire, only finer and newer, when the wearer could afford this. We will give you just a few ideas below; for more information on Irish wedding fashions please see Chapter 6.

In the nineteenth century, Irish society was, broadly speaking, divided into two classes: the aristocratic and the farming class. Only very wealthy brides could afford to wear the kind of white gown that was made popular by Queen Victoria. A farmer's bride would have chosen something that could be worn again, often a two-piece of a skirt and blouse with a jacket or a nice dress, while men wore their best suits.

At the beginning of the twentieth century, wedding fashions became more relaxed and sometimes even whimsical and frivolous.

At the end of the marriage rite, the couple had to circle the altar three times, after which the veil would be lifted and the couple would seal their vows with a kiss.

While having a veil embroidered by hand is quite costly, it may be worth it if you would like your veil to be an heirloom that can be worn by other members of your family and passed down from generation to generation. Lace can also be used as an embellishment on the gown itself.

Needlepoint and bobbin lace-making were introduced to Ireland in the seventeenth century, probably by nuns who lived in monasteries that had affiliations with monasteries in France. Lace-making would appear to have expanded during the Famine, when nuns taught local women how to make lace in order to give them a means of making a living. Lace-making was at its most popular between 1900 and 1914. It peaked in 1907, according to Ada Longfeld's *Irish Lace*. As the great craftswomen grew older and died, the tradition died with them in the early twentieth century. Today there has been a revival of sorts, and if you are interested in having your wedding gown embellished with lace, you will be able to find or commission it in County Monaghan (the lace-making county of Ireland) at the Clones Lace Guild. The guild takes commissions for pieces of lace and lace veils. If you are interested in learning more about Irish lace, there is also a Lace Museum in the village of Banaleck, which also has a shop that sells antique lace. Carrickmacross lace is also very popular today, as is Kenmare lace, made in Kenmare, County Kerry. If you do decide to commission lace for your gown or veil, allow about three months for a veil and a little less for a smaller piece.

Tiaras or 'minns' are also popular accessories for brides. According to Shannon McMahon Lichte, Celtic men and women

Brides often wore hats instead of veils, and lace and flowy
replaced stiffer fabrics like satin. This trend continued un
Second World War, when most Irish women wore a simpl
as there was little money for lavish weddings. Today, Irish w
tend to favour wearing white gowns on their wedding days a

Some brides now also opt for gowns that are inspired by
Celts. While they can often be very beautiful, it has to be said t
it is usually brides who are of Irish extraction, not brides born a
raised in Ireland, who go for this type of dress. There are desig
who specialise in these types of gowns, and more information ca
be found at the back of the book in the Useful Websites section.

Often, a skilled seamstress will also be able to replicate a gown
that could have been worn by a Celtic bride.

If you would like to incorporate Irish or Celtic decoration
in a subtler way, you could have a look at embroidery – any
kind of Celtic design can be embroidered onto the bodice of
your gown or along the sleeves or hem of the dress, as well a
on the veil. Embroidery on wedding attire has a long histo.
that includes Queen Victoria, who had her wedding dre
embroidered with symbols for each of her kingdoms (the Tud
rose for England, the leek for Wales, the shamrock for Irelan
and the thistle for Scotland). You could also look to Irish danci
competition outfits for inspiration, but remember that these
themselves 'inspired' by Celtic designs and can often be qu
garish – perhaps not the look you are going for with a weddi
dress.

For many of us, the quintessential bridal accessory is the v
Originally worn to protect the bride from evil spirits, they a
came to represent purity and chastity. According to Lady Wil
couples in rural Ireland used to be veiled in heavy black cloth
the beginning of the ceremony to represent the mystery of lov

of higher classes used to wear a crown, commonly known as a 'minn', for special occasions. For inspiration you could have a look at a thirteenth-century fresco painting of the O'Connors, kings of Connaught, which shows these decorated Irish crowns on the heads of the clan's leaders. Today you can get tiaras with many different designs and produced in all sorts of materials. If you like, you can even get tiaras that are inspired by the *Book of Kells*.

If you are getting married in the winter, you could also have a cape made for you, like the Kinsale or Kerry cloak. This is a full-length cloak with a hood, and was worn by country women in the west of Ireland in the 1800s. It was traditionally made of water-resistant lamb's wool, but today you can have one made in silk or velvet in a variety of colours. Red was a particularly popular colour in Galway.

If you are superstitious, you should probably know that it used to be considered lucky to get married in an old pair of shoes. What better excuse to buy a gorgeous pair now and wear them out for a couple of months before the wedding? There are different explanations for this – in Cork it was believed that fairies would whisk away a bride and groom to Tír na n'Og just to get their hands on a new pair of slippers, so this risk could be minimised by either not buying a new pair at all or by wearing a new pair in (inconspicuously and safely) well before the wedding. This superstition might also come from the idea that it is good to begin a new journey with something familiar, like a favourite pair of shoes. It's a useful custom to hang on to either way, because you need to break your shoes in before the day, or your feet will be killing you before you even make it out of the church. If you would rather wear a brand-new pair to your wedding, you can incorporate this custom in a different way – you could tie a pair of old shoes to the back of the newlyweds' car – leather is thought to offer protection from evil spirits, and shoes are thought, for some reason, to ensure fertility.

In the Cork countryside it is believed that the last stitch of a bride's wedding dress should be sewn on the morning of the wedding to ensure a lucky marriage. This can be done by stitching a little blue ribbon (something blue) or piece of fabric from the bride's mother's gown (something old) to the inside of the dress. It is also believed that a bride who sews the last few stitches of her gown makes her happiness complete, so she should be the one to sew that last stitch.

Finally, here are a few more superstitions that apply to the bridal outfit. While we can't be sure that they all originated in

Ireland, it will probably do no harm to keep them in mind, as you can never have too much good luck on your wedding day.

When the bride gets dressed, she should make sure there are no pins left stuck in her gown, or she will experience misfortune in her married life.

A spider hidden in the fabric of the bride's dress will bring her wealth.

A bride should not try on her entire wedding ensemble before the wedding day. It is considered presumptuous to do so, and would therefore be tempting fate.

Flowers

There are many flowers that are indigenous to Ireland and, if you wanted to, you could quite easily put together a bouquet that is made up entirely of Irish flowers. In the Middle Ages, it was believed that herbs would ward off evil spirits, so brides would carry bouquets of herbs on their wedding day to ensure safety. Men going into battle would also pin their lady's colours close to their heart using a flower, which is where the groom's boutonniere comes from. The Victorians expanded upon this and assigned meaning to many flowers, which were then used by courting couples.

Some Irish flowers you might consider using include:

Burnet Rose – a white rose that grows wild all over Ireland and symbolizes respect.

Violets – symbolise faithfulness, and the common wild variety is indigenous to Ireland.

Hydrangea – stands for devotion and remembrance, and is found in pink and blue all over the west of Ireland.

Pansy – this flower says that the wearer is having 'thoughts of you' and the delicate seaside pansy can be found in Ireland.

Foxglove – if you feel like being a fairy queen for a day, the Irish for foxglove, *lus na mban síde*, translates as 'plant of the fairy women'.

Daisy – this little flower represents innocence, and the ox-eye variety grows wild all over Ireland.

Elderberry – the 'wildflower of Ireland' represents warmth and kindness.

Irish Orchids – stand for lust and luxury. That doesn't really fit in with the very chaste and pure look most brides seem to go for now, but maybe more modern and adventurous brides won't be bothered by that.

Primrose – is also indigenous to Ireland and wards off evil. According to Lady Wilde, 'evil spirits cannot touch anything guarded by primroses, if they are plucked before sunrise.'

Ferns – symbolise sincerity and were used in medieval love potions. Killarney ferns are grown in Ireland.

Ivy – is symbolic of wedded love and can be found all over Ireland.

If you are looking for more inspiration or for something a little different to include in your bouquet, you could use a sprig of mint. As we saw earlier, according to Lady Wilde, if you hold a sprig of mint until it grows moist and then clasp the hand of your intended, the love will be returned as long as the two hands are closed over the herb, so you could tuck a sprig of mint into the bridal bouquet.

You could also use shamrock, which was used by St Patrick to explain the Holy Trinity to the Irish. According to Irish legend, each leaf of the lucky four-leafed variety has a special meaning, all of which are quite appropriate for the wedding day ...

One leaf for Hope, the second for Faith,
The third for Love, and the fourth for Luck!

Shamrock should probably be used in moderation though, as it is only really used decoratively in Ireland around St Patrick's Day and could look a little silly if it was overdone at a wedding at a different time of year.

We also saw earlier that there is a custom that comes from the farming community in Northern Ireland, where young men and women would take long plaits of straw and twist them into love knots. These harvest knots would then be given as love tokens to be worn on a lapel. Women could also wear these knots woven into their hair, and giving a harvest knot to a lover was considered a sign of commitment. If you would like to use a harvest knot, or love knot, it could be attached to the groom's lapel as a boutonniere, or part of one. It could also be incorporated into the bride's headdress, whether it be a veil, a hat, or a floral wreath.

Getting There

Once the bride is dressed and has her bouquet, it's time to get to the church or registry office. If you are interested in getting to your wedding in a uniquely Irish form of transport, you might want to investigate the possibility of organising jaunting carts, which were used on the Aran Islands. This was mostly for practical reasons, however, as there are very few cars on the Aran Islands. You could probably use a horse-drawn carriage instead, though this is less 'authentic' and wouldn't have been an option available to the majority of Irish brides in the days when these carriages were commonly used. Another, more common option, would be to walk to the church.

Decorative Touches

Your invitations give your guests an initial impression of the kind of wedding you are having, and if you would like to make it clear that you are having an 'Irish' wedding it could be a nice touch to have invitations that are decorated with Celtic art from illuminated gospels like the *Book of Kells*. If you are artistic and decide to have a go at making these yourself, try to go back to photo facsimiles of the original manuscripts, available in many Irish bookshops and online. Art that is 'inspired by' these manuscripts tends to be quite derivative and is aimed mainly at tourists. You can also find stationers who specialise in these kinds of invitations, and many 'regular' stationers in Ireland now stock a range of Celtic-design invitations.

If you are of Irish descent and can trace your origins back to a particular family, you may want to use your family coat of arms.

For more information, please refer to the Useful Websites section at the back of the book.

Once the invitations have been sent out, the next thing your guests will see of your wedding will be the place where you have your ceremony. If you would like to welcome your guests to the ceremony in an old-fashioned way, you could use the following custom. During the nineteenth century in Ireland, the entire village would sometimes get involved in a wedding, especially if the couple came from a family of high social standing. On the morning of the big day, the inhabitants of the village would decorate the path from the bride's house to the church with flower garlands or boughs that would arch across the couple's path. Sometimes there would also be lanterns or burning torches. If you are lucky enough to be getting married in a church or other venue that is close enough for you to walk to, you could ask friends and family to do this for you, perhaps on a smaller scale. Decorating the path with lights and lanterns can also be done on a smaller scale by even just lining the couple's path with candles and flowers, as is done in many churches.

If you are having a religious ceremony you may want to include Celtic crosses as part of your decor, which can easily be found in gift shops and jewellers in Ireland.

You could also get a harpist to play during the ceremony, but the delicate music of the harp might be lost in the din at the reception. The harp is the national symbol of Ireland, and has been associated with the country for centuries. Images of harps can be found carved on Irish stones that date back to the twelfth century. In ancient Ireland, professional harpists were honoured above all other musicians. Irish harpists often played before the high chiefs of Ireland. The harp that is used as the model for the harps found on Irish Euro coins and as the official symbol of Ireland is the fourteenth-century harp that is now preserved in the museum of Trinity College, Dublin. The harp, again, should be used in moderation if used as a decorative motif, or it may look like the Irish Tourism Board had a hand in decorating your church or reception venue.

You could also be inspired by Celtic myths or legends (swans are very popular in Celtic mythology), and you could use Irish linen and crystal, or Irish flowers to decorate your church and as centrepieces.

All the days of our life ...

A tradition has developed of the bride being late for the ceremony. While this is acceptable when she is ten to fifteen minutes late, anything more than that is generally considered bad form. The authors have yet to find a tradition or superstition that justifies keeping one's guests waiting any longer than this.

Once she has arrived at the church the bride faces that long walk down the aisle. If she finds herself overcome with emotion she can always carry with her a linen handkerchief – a tradition that was probably started by the linen industry in Northern Ireland. It is good luck, by the way, to cry before the wedding – according to Irish folklore it means that there will be no tears after the wedding. If you decide to carry a linen handkerchief, you can turn it into an heirloom with a few stitches, transforming   it into a christening bonnet for your first child. It can then be turned back into a handkerchief with a few snips, for the child to carry on his/her wedding day, tucked into a pocket or wrapped around the bouquet.

If you would like to remember someone who has passed away, there are two ways of doing this that are rooted in Irish customs.

Loved ones who have passed away are honoured on two days of the year in Ireland – on Garland Sunday, the first Sunday in September, and on All Souls' Day, 2 November.

On All Souls' Day a candle is put in the window of the home for each person who has passed, so that they can find their way home to visit on this one day in the year. Celebrating Garland Sunday is an ancient Celtic custom. A hoop or wreath made of twigs was decorated with flowers and ribbons by unmarried girls (because it was believed that the touch of a married woman's hand would bring bad luck) and these garlands would be left at burial sites and prayers would be said over them. Both of these customs can be incorporated in a wedding ceremony by lighting candles and by placing small floral garlands around these candles. Obviously, in Christian ceremonies there are similar ways of remembering the dead during the service.

If you are not having a Christian service, or if your officiant is open to incorporating old Celtic elements in your ceremony, you could also include a ritual called the Caim. The following is an extract from Shannon McMahon Lichte's *Irish Wedding Traditions*:

> The Caim is an early Celtic Christian custom that can be used to begin an Irish wedding ceremony. Celtic Christians would draw

a circle around themselves as a sign of unity with God. The circle was a symbol of the encircling of God's love and the "Mighty Three". The following incantation has multiple meanings. It refers to the Father, Son, and Holy Spirit, as well as the trinity of sky, earth, and water, which are three sacred elements in Celtic tradition. This prayer, from David Adam's book *The Eye of the Eagle*, can be repeated as the circle is drawn.

A Caim Prayer
The Mighty Three,
My protection be.
Encircling me.
You are around,
My life,
My love,
My home,
Encircling me.
O sacred Three,
The Mighty Three.[19]

Many couples will give each other a coin at some point during their wedding ceremony to show symbolically that from now on their property is shared, that everything that is his is hers and vice versa. This used to be done on the Aran Islands, where a man would give his bride a silver coin to symbolise this and also that the couple hoped for wealth – both material and spiritual – in their married life. Today the bride would usually give the groom a coin too, so that the exchange is more equal. These kinds of wedding coins can be bought from jewellers, and some jewellers supply them for free when you buy your wedding bands. You can also exchange a different gift if you prefer, such as jewellery. If you decide to give each other a coin, it's nice to give an old coin, like a silver crown or an Irish £1 Millennium coin.

The tokens are generally exchanged with these words:

I give you this gift as a token of all that I possess.

Some couples also choose to have verses of poetry read during the ceremony, and there is a wealth of Irish poetry to choose from. Again, if you are having a religious ceremony make sure that the poetry is appropriate by checking with your officiant first.

Another old Irish tradition is to have the officiant bless a little silver bell which the bride and groom then give a good shake to while thinking lovingly of each other and of their future. The bell is then taken home and left in a handy spot where it can be picked up whenever an argument arises. The bell is used to call a truce and is supposed to bring back happy memories and remind the couple of how much they love each other, and of the vows they made to each other on their wedding day. This custom appears to come from a peasant tradition from the west of Ireland, where the bell is called St Patrick's Bell of Will. St Patrick often used bells and believed that they helped him to perform miracles. He is said to have been buried with the Bell of Will, which was later exhumed and is today displayed in the National Museum.

If the couple wish to involve their mothers in the ceremony, they can do so by asking them to present to the couple a cross of St Brigid. St Brigid's day is on 1 February. Born in 452, she was baptised by St Patrick and entered religious life, and many miracles are attributed to her. Brigid was the patron saint to the Knights of Chivalry and legend has it that the knights

began the custom of calling the girls they married 'brides' after St Brigid. Brigid is known as the patron saint of protection, and St Brigid's crosses are put up in homes all around Ireland to invoke her protection. It is believed that she converted a pagan to Christianity on his deathbed by plaiting rushes she found near the dying man's bed into the shape of the Cross of Calvary. When hung in the home, St Brigid's crosses are thought to protect the house against fire and the elements, as well as to protect the occupants from sickness and disease. They also keep out evil spirits. Married couples used to be presented with a cross for their new homes by their mothers, and they would add one more cross for every year they lived in this home. The crosses were presented by their mothers because the home is associated with mothers, and nowadays this could be incorporated just after the wedding ceremony.

In Limerick, in the early twentieth century, children would wait outside churches for the bridal party to emerge because the guests gathered there would throw coins at the new couple and the children would grab the money. There was a superstition that not giving to the poor would make you unlucky in your marriage, so this probably evolved from newlyweds giving money to poor people outside the church after services. If you wanted to do something similar, you could make a donation to a charity whose work you support. Increasingly, couples are making a donation to the charity of their choice in each of their guests' names instead of giving guests a favour – which is not an Irish tradition anyway, as far as we could ascertain. In many European countries, the traditional favour is a little bag filled with five sugared almonds, representing good health, wealth, happiness, fertility and longevity.

The Wedding Feast

Hospitality has always been very important in Ireland, and it continues to be as important in Irish culture today as it was centuries ago. According to Brehon laws, hospitality was considered the duty of each individual, and it was a crime not to offer food and drink to any person who came to visit or who was passing in their travels.

Food is an especially important element of hospitality, not only at Irish weddings, but at most weddings in most cultures. The quality of the food (unlike the colour of the tablerunners) will be noticed by everyone and is one of the things people tend to remember about weddings they attend.

As for good Irish food – if you're in Ireland your best bet is usually to choose food that is locally produced and in season, as well as food for the quality of which Ireland is famous – beef, lamb, mussels, oysters, and salmon, to name but a few. Unless

you are catering for a small group of people whose tastes you know, the simpler the food is, the better. If you are having an autumn or winter wedding you could consider serving dishes like colcannon or Irish stew, but these dishes are often not considered fancy enough for a wedding and wouldn't really be served much anymore at contemporary Irish weddings.

Irish wedding cake is traditionally a fruitcake that is filled with raisins, currants, almonds, and other rich, dried fruits. It is iced with almond paste and sugar icing, which helps to keep it from going off. The richness of the cake is thought to symbolise future prosperity for the couple, as well as representing fertility. When the cake is cut and shared, the bride and groom are sharing their prosperity and happiness with their guests. Some couples send slices to guests who are unable to attend, sharing their happiness with them, too – fruitcake keeps very well, so there is no danger of it going stale in the post. If you decide to have a fruitcake, you should serve thin slices of it because it's a very rich cake. Irish couples often used to save the top tier of the cake for the baptism of their first child, and if you choose to do this make sure you store it properly.

If the bride doesn't have as good a relationship with her mother-in-law as she might wish for, it can also be a good idea for the mother-in-law to crumble some of the first slice of the cake over the bride's head, as this is thought to ensure that they will have a good relationship, but this can also be done when the bride and groom first enter their new home.

If you would like to have an Irish beverage on offer that isn't Guinness or whiskey, you could consider serving meade – 'the oldest drink in Ireland'. It used to be consumed to promote virility and was sometimes drank for a whole month after the wedding, as explained in Chapter 4 – hence the term 'honeymoon'.

There is also a tradition in many cultures of the husband and wife sharing a glass or cup for their first drink. You could use a ceremonial cup like a quaich or some Irish crystal to do this the Irish way. The idea is that the cup or glass is passed down from generation to generation, ensuring happiness and good fortune for all who drink from it.

Music and Entertainment

There is no shortage of beautiful Irish music that can be played both during the wedding ceremony and later at the reception. When choosing songs remember to check if they are really as appropriate as they might at first seem. *She Moved Through the Fair*, for example, while very beautiful, is actually about a bride who dies before her wedding day. Also keep in mind that some churches will not allow you to play music in the church or at certain points during the ceremony that is not sacred. This is why many churches don't allow Wagner's *Bridal March* ('Here Comes the Bride') to be played – because it is from an opera called *Lohengrin*.

Centuries ago, the bridal party would often walk in a procession to and from the church led by a fiddler, who would play tunes to get everyone in a festive mood. One such tune would be *Haste to the Wedding*. You could also have someone play the uilleann pipes – though they tend to be an acquired taste.

As we mentioned earlier, when the couple take to the floor for their first dance, the groom should make sure that the bride doesn't take both of her feet off the floor, or the fairies will spirit her away. The song for the first dance is usually chosen for its associations and memories for the couple, but it could also be an Irish tune.

If you enjoy Irish dancing, you might also consider having a group of dancers perform at the reception, or you could try to get your guests to do some dancing themselves by providing the soundtrack – either live or from a recording.

It tends to be a feature of Irish weddings that guests like to get up and sing, and this can be great if you are expecting it or are happy for it to happen. If, however, an unruly guest takes over the microphone completely, you should have an emergency plan in place.

We have already mentioned the garter and bouquet tosses in previous chapters, so we will simply reiterate that it is up to each individual couple to decide if they want to do this or not.

As discussed in an earlier chapter, strawboys would often put in an appearance at Irish country weddings until the middle of the last century. This is becoming quite rare now, but if you wanted your friends to re-enact something along these lines for you, perhaps you could leave this book lying around – open at the appropriate page – when they call over to see you in the weeks and months before you get married.

Another amusing feature of Irish weddings, which originated relatively recently in Cork and seems to be growing in popularity, is the 'Whiskey Walk'. Bottles of whiskey are placed on each table, and as the groom makes the rounds of the room, saying hello to all of his guests, he has to drink a toast from the bottle on the table. It is highly recommended that he paces himself and takes his time.

In the unlikely event that your guests might get a little bored after all that, you could suggest an old favourite from Irish country weddings called 'Kick the Turnip', which consisted of doing precisely that. Unfortunately, the authors could not unearth the precise rules according to which this game is played, but perhaps an imaginative groom can come up with a new set of rules to delight his friends and new wife on the day.

In the nineteenth and early twentieth centuries there would have been a lot of merrymaking on the way home from the wedding, as well as at the wedding. Men would race each other and compete in various games, and the winner would get a bottle of whiskey from the bride. Perhaps it was in order to avoid this mayhem after a long day that couples began to take a different path home from the one they had taken to the wedding. Many pranks would have been played on the new couple, but as well as avoiding this, they may also have wanted to avoid being whisked away by fairies (who, as noted elsewhere already, were particularly keen on brides in their fine dress). The couple was also symbolically forging a new path together, so it was appropriate to take a different road home together.

For some of the pranks that were played on newlyweds, please see Chapter 4.

Most Irish couples did not traditionally go on a honeymoon until quite recently, when travel became affordable for many people. For most, it was straight back to work after the festivities. If you don't live in Ireland and decide to visit on your honeymoon, make sure you come prepared for the weather!

When the Honeymoon is Over …

Up until the late nineteenth century, it was believed that no one should enter their home without salt, a broom and holy water: salt has always been associated with keeping away evil; brooms have long been a symbol of domesticity and any future sadness that might come into the house can be swept away with a daily swish of the broom; and finally, holy water is a daily reminder of a family's faith in God. A newlywed woman should carry these items across the threshold as she enters her home for the first time – preferably in the arms of her new husband, as carrying the bride over the threshold is thought to trick the little people, who are lying in wait, ready to spirit the new wife away.

There was a belief among the Celts that when a fire was lit and burned for three days straight, the home and land upon which the fire burned would become one with the people who lit the flame. To do this nowadays you would need a very big, long-burning candle, or a large fireplace. Please make sure that it is 100 per cent safe to do this before you attempt this at home.

Another charming if pricey custom that you might like to follow is the one of making the flowers of the bride's bouquet the official 'flowers of the home'. When entertaining, a bowl or vase of the bride's signature flowers would grace the table. While not always feasible, this could be a nice touch for special occasions, to remind you both of the joy of your wedding day.

Conclusion

We hope that you have enjoyed taking this journey down memory lane through Irish wedding customs as much as we have enjoyed researching it. From proposals to keeping the home safe from fire and ill health, we hope we have given you some idea of how Irish couples who came before you found their match and got them up the aisle and safely home.

With all the pressures of modern life, wedding planning can sometimes seem like just one more stressful chore to get through for many couples. With the words of wisdom, superstitions and trivia about weddings contained in this book, we hope to have informed, inspired and, above all, amused you, and to have put some of the things that stress couples out into a little bit of perspective.

Planning a wedding can quite quickly come to seem like a full-time job, but it really need not be. As long as you keep your sense of perspective and humour intact throughout, you may even enjoy the weird and wonderful world of Irish weddings.

As with any book that collects folklore and traditions – many of which have survived and been handed down through the generations in various different versions and forms – it is impossible to include everything, or to guarantee the 'authenticity' of all the customs described herein. While a source may tell us that a certain custom originated in Ireland, the author of this source often would have had their information from a person in the community, who can only confirm the accuracy of this information as far back as living memory allows. We hope that we have not included as 'Irish' a tradition that is actually Scottish or English (or from even further afield), but if so, we welcome clarification from our readers. We also welcome any additional information or corrections the attentive reader may be able to point out to us.

We both have many people to thank for helping us to put this book together, both collectively and individually. We would like to thank Nonsuch for offering us the opportunity to write this book. We would also like to thank our editor Jenna Cattermole for all her hard work and invaluable suggestions and insights.

Bridgette would like to thank her family and friends for their support and encouragement during her period in captivity whilst writing this book. In particular, she would like to thank her boyfriend Michael for not getting too alarmed by her incessant talk of weddings and for being so helpful and understanding at all times. Finally, she would like to dedicate this book to her late grandmother Sarah Rowland, whose voracious appetite for books single-handedly kept her local mobile library in business; her love of literature was just one of the many gifts she imparted to her granddaugher.

Kerstin would like to thank Alessandro for listening to far more wedding-related chat than it is reasonable to expect any man to put up with. She would also like to thank her family and friends for their constructive criticism and feedback. Their confidence in her ability to write this book often exceeded her own. She hopes that the result will not disappoint them. Finally, she would like to dedicate this book to her grandmothers, two very formidable ladies whose style and class she aspires to one day emulate.

Bibliography

Ballard, Linda May. *Forgetting Frolic: Marriage Traditions in Ireland*. Belfast, 1998

Bluett, Anthony. *Ireland in Love*. Dublin, 1995

Buckley, Maria. *Irish Marriage Customs*. Cork, 2000

Colum, Padraic. *A Treasury of Irish Folklore*. New York, 1983

Croker, T.C. *Fairy Legends II*. Cork, 1998

Danahar, Kevin. *The Year in Ireland*. Cork, 1972

Delamore, Philip. *The Wedding Dress: A Sourcebook*. London, 2005

Fallon, Rosaleen. *A County Roscommon Wedding 1892: The Marriage of John Hughes and Mary Gavin*. Dublin, 2004

Fielding, William J. *Strange Customs of Courtship and Marriage*. New York, 1942

Forden, Diane. *Bridal Guide® Magazine's New Etiquette for Today's Bride*. New York, 2004

Guth, Tracy. *I Do: A Book for Brides*. Kansas City, 2000

Longfeld, Ada. *Irish Lace*. Dublin, 1978

Mac a'Bháird, Natasha. *The Irish Bride's Survival Guide: Plan Your Perfect Wedding*. Dublin, 2005

McGuire, Kim. *Irish Love and Wedding Traditions*. Dublin, 2000

McGart, Billy. *Poor Rabbin's Ollminick for the Town of Belfast, 1861*. Belfast, 1861

McNamara, Marie and Madden, Maura. *Irish Folklore Commission: Beagh a History and Heritage*. Beagh, 1995

Messenger, B. *Picking up the Linen Threads*. Austin and London, 1975

O'Farrell, Padraic. *Irish Customs*. Dublin, 2004

Wilde, Lady. *Ancient Cures, Charms and Usages*. London, 1880

Wilde, Lady. *Ancient Legends of Ireland*. London, 1888

Wilde, Lady. *Irish Cures, Mystic Charms and Superstitions*. Cork and Dublin, 1988

-----. *Tying the Knot: Marriage Traditions in the North of Ireland*. Belfast,
    The Ulster Folk and Transport Museum, date unknown.

Useful Websites

Websites tend to evolve quite quickly so we would like to point out that we cannot guarantee that any of the information you find on them will be 100 per cent accurate. And do be careful on the internet – never, ever give out any personal information on a wedding website, no matter how friendly it may seem. They can be accessed by any member of the general public at any time. Please also note that we do not endorse these sites or businesses, we have merely found them to be useful to ourselves and other brides in the past.

www. weddingsonline.ie – this is a good resource for Irish suppliers and has links to some really great Irish designers, etc.

www. simplyweddings.ie – the authors are not very familiar with this site themselves, but it comes recommended by other Irish brides.

www. gettingmarried.ie – this is a Catholic website and will help you to plan your ceremony. It has a really useful tool for putting booklets together.

www. confetti.co.uk – this site has some useful planning tools, including a seating planner – what more could a bride ask for?

www. oasis.gov – this site has a section that explains the legal aspects of getting married in Ireland.

www. groni.gov.uk – has the same type of information for Northern Ireland.

www. theknot.com – has a huge selection of beautiful photographs (particularly of flowers and gowns) to inspire you.

www. weddingchannel.com – has useful tools like a free wedding website builder and budgeter, etc.

www. brides.com – the *Community* section on this site is very helpful, as there tend to be people there who really know their music, readings, etc.

www. irishsurnames.com – this site might help you to find your family coat of arms.

Endnotes

1   Fallon, Rosaleen. *A County Roscommon Wedding 1892: The Marriage of John Hughes and Mary Gavin*, p. 29

2   Buckley, Maria. *Irish Marriage Customs*, Cork, Mercier Press, 2000. p. 33

3   McNamara, Marie and Madden, Maura. *Irish Folklore Commission, Beagh a History and Heritage*, Beagh 1995, p. 203

4   Buckley, Maria. *Irish Marriage Customs*, p. 22

5   Danaher, Kevin. *The Year in Ireland*, Mercier Press, 1972, p. 51

6   *Journal of the Cork and Archaeological Society*, 1895, p. 420

7   Danaher, Kevin. *The Year in Ireland*, Mercier Press, 1972, p. 50

8   McGuire, Kim. *Irish Love and Wedding Customs*. p. 39

9   Ballard, Linda May. *Forgetting Frolic: Marriage Traditions in Ireland*. p. 122

10 Messenger, B. *Picking up the Linen Threads*, Austin and London. 1975, p. 174

11 Ballard, Linda May. *Forgetting Frolic: Marriage Traditions in Ireland*. Belfast: The Institute of Irish Studies and Folklore Society, 1998. p. 77

12 Ballard, Linda May. *Forgetting Frolic: Marriage Traditions in Ireland*. Belfast: The Institute of Irish Studies and Folklore Society, 1998. p. 78

13 Delamore, Philip. *The Wedding Dress: A Sourcebook*. London: Pavilion Books, 2005. p. 54

14 Ballard, Linda May. *Forgetting Frolic: Marriage Traditions in Ireland*. Belfast: The Institute of Irish Studies and Folklore Society, 1998. p. 81

15   Ballard, Linda May. *Forgetting Frolic: Marriage Traditions in Ireland.* Belfast:
      The Institute of Irish Studies and Folklore Society, 1998.p. 77
·16   Ballard, Linda May. *Forgetting Frolic: Marriage Traditions in Ireland.* Belfast:
      The Institute of Irish Studies and Folklore Society, 1998. p. 89
17   Mac a'Bháird, Natasha. *The Irish Bride's Survival Guide: Plan Your Perfect
      Wedding.* Dublin: O'Brien Press, 2005. p. 200
18   McMahon Lichte, Shannon. *Irish Wedding Traditions: Using Your Irish Heritage
      to Create the Perfect Wedding*, New York: Hyperion, 2001. p. 44
19   McMahon Lichte, Shannon. *Irish Wedding Traditions: Using Your Irish Heritage
      to Create the Perfect Wedding*, New York: Hyperion, 2001. p. 72